MW01169423

SUITED FOR
SUCCESS
VOLUME 2

SUITED FOR
SUCCESS
VOLUME 2

25 Inspirational Stories on Getting
Prepared for Your Journey to Success

PK KERSEY

purposely
created
PUBLISHING

SUITED FOR SUCCESS, VOLUME 2
Published by Purposely Created Publishing Group™
Copyright © 2019 PK Kersey
All rights reserved.

No part of this book may be reproduced, distributed or transmitted in any form by any means, graphic, electronic, or mechanical, including photocopy, recording, taping, or by any information storage or retrieval system, without permission in writing from the publisher, except in the case of reprints in the context of reviews, quotes, or references.

Printed in the United States of America
ISBN: 978-1-64484-109-9

Special discounts are available on bulk quantity purchases by book clubs, associations and special interest groups. For details email: sales@publishyourgift.com or call (888) 949-6228.

For information logon to:
www.PublishYourGift.com

Table of Contents

Introduction

Welcome to *Suited for Success, Volume 2*! I am so happy that you have decided to support us. So many people were blessed by *Suited for Success, Volume 1* that I decided to continue with another book. I believe that representation matters and what better way to show the next generation what great things men of color are doing than to write about them. As you sit down and read the fantastic stories of these great men, I believe they will inspire you. We normally only hear the stories of the actor or the athlete, but *Suited for Success* allows us to hear the stories of our fathers, brothers, and uncles. How they fought challenges, stood on faith, and would not quit. Men of color are living their dreams every day and I feel it is the right time to start celebrating them. Once again, welcome...

Live Life as if You Could Fail

PK Kersey

I know that title sounds and looks like a typo. Usually when you hear this statement it is said like this: "Live life as if you could not fail." I totally understand what is meant when this is said. The implication is to do what you dream about doing and act like failure is not an option. I get it. Believe me I do; however, to me that does not have the same impact. I want people to really understand and embrace the fact that failure is very real. So real in fact that it should not be avoided or feared but quite the opposite. It should be embraced and anticipated because in doing so I have found out so much about myself through the many failures I have faced. Not only that, but because of each failure I have come out stronger, more focused, and determined to be even better than ever. Now I know that sounds like just another corny motivational saying but let me tell you that this is true. Failure turns out to be a blessing after it is finished with you. Like so many other things I can think of it is terrible initially, but we are better because of it. I drink apple cider vinegar, honey, and lemon juice every morning. When I first drink it, it tastes horrible. However, I know my body is better off because of it. Also, I exercise often. My body definitely doesn't want to at first, but I love the benefits of exercising after I am done. So, failure has to be viewed the same way. I don't want to fail but I now know that WHEN I do, I am helping my future self greatly. I believe that God makes great people, but sometimes those great people make the tough decisions to be mediocre.

What Is Failure?

Webster defines failure as: a lack of success. Kersey defines failure as: a process of success. Due to the way Webster defines failure, it is no wonder most people want to avoid it at all costs. If you believe in your mind that failure is truly a lack of success and not a process to achieving success, then that makes sense. Just say it to yourself slowly...

Lack of success. Wait 10 seconds and then say: Process of success. Just saying it and then meditating over it will begin to change your thought process concerning failure. It won't be such a dirty word in your mind when you do that. As simple as that sounds, this is a critical step to take on the journey to becoming successful. As a movie buff, I remember a scene in the movie *A Vampire in Brooklyn*, with Eddie Murphy. His character, Preacher Pauly, was preaching a sermon and he was trying to convince the congregation that evil was good. These churchgoers had never heard this before so Preacher Pauly had to convince them to change their minds concerning evil. All their lives they were taught that evil was bad, but now this preacher was coming against one of their core values. So, in order for Pauly to convince them he had them repeat after him a few times that evil was good. After they said it a few times, he saw them begin to change their thinking. Well, that is what I am doing right now. Failure is good, failure is a process, failure is not evil, failure doesn't mean God doesn't love you, failure doesn't mean final, failure doesn't mean it's over.

Failure is a lesson that must be learned. Don't take this lightly, as this lesson must be learned to change your thinking about failure.

Study any successful person and you will find a tremendous amount of failures in their past. In fact, most times they will talk about their failures more than their successes because usually they remember those times more.

Teachers of the great inventor Thomas Edison said he was too stupid to learn anything, he was fired from jobs for being non-productive, and it took him 1,000 attempts to perfect the lightbulb.

Michael Jordan was cut from his HS team and is known for his statement, "I failed over and over again in my life. That is why I succeed."

F.W. Woolworth was not allowed to wait on customers because his boss said that he didn't have enough sense. Ironically, I actually worked in a Woolworth store in downtown Brooklyn while in college; it was my first job.

Oprah Winfrey grew up poor and was molested and raped as a child. Also, as a teenager she was pregnant with a son who was born prematurely and died. She was also told she would never make it as a TV host.

Steve Harvey was homeless, Lebron James grew up without his dad, and the list goes on and on.

Now remember Webster's definition of failure as a lack of success? When you think of these individuals, the last thing you think about is a lack of success despite all of these failures. However, the failures played a huge role in the process of success in their lives.

What Is Success?

Now that we have addressed failure, we also have to talk about success. Another important ingredient for being successful is being able to identify what success is to you. Not what your parents tell you it is, or your friends tell you it is, but what you believe it is. That is critical because if you try to be successful based on someone else's definition, you will be frustrated and unfulfilled. So, think about what you would define success as. Make sure it is not someone else's definition but yours. This was a very challenging process for me because I had excellent examples. My parents worked for companies in NYC for over 24 years each and retired. They owned a beautiful home with two cars. They had set an example of success. That was their definition and I followed it. I worked for a company for 24 years with plans to retire. However, I was very unhappy and unfulfilled there because that was not my definition of success. I had neglected to define success for myself. I had only replicated my parents' definition. Yes, it worked wonderfully for them but not for me. Not at all.

How could it? It was not what I wanted. Even though I had not yet defined what success was for me, somehow, I knew what it wasn't. It wasn't doing the same reports over and over again.

It wasn't having to report to a supervisor who severely lacked people skills. It definitely wasn't not receiving a raise for over three years. It also wasn't working behind a desk not being able to use my creativity. So, I knew what it wasn't but that is not good enough. I had to know more than that to direct my energy. I had to know what it was.

I began experimenting with other opportunities to help me define success. I tried working with multi-level marketing companies. I always saw people make money with those companies, but I never did. I would try to follow the rules and advice of the leaders but never seemed to prosper with them. I worked in about four MLM companies in total but never accomplished anything worthwhile. They all seemed to begin with so much promise but for whatever reason they never took off.

Then, I partnered with my brother and a friend of mine and started a chair rental company, which lasted about two years. We were fortunate enough to be given over 100 chairs and decided to rent them out to companies to make some income. It started out well. We acquired a solid client. Unfortunately, they soon stopped paying and fell on hard times.

That resulted in the company being evicted from the building they were using and losing all of their possessions, including our chairs. That was devastating to us. That along with differences among the partners regarding the direction of the business resulted in us shutting down.

I then was asked to purchase a few vending machines and place them in different locations in the city, but I could never seem to get that off the ground. After talking about doing that for about a year, I changed my direction and decided to write a book.

While working for the NYS DMV on 34th. Street in NYC, I would go out for lunch and write outside while enjoying the excellent weather and watching crowds of people walk by. I love the city and would walk to Bryant Park for inspiration for my first book. I really enjoyed the process of putting the story together page by page. That was the summer of 2008. I remember it like it was yesterday. Day after day, walking nine blocks to the park and then back to work, it was really coming together. I felt that once the book was completed, it was going to be my big break. But then something happened. Something called life. Work got hectic. Fall and winter came, and I couldn't walk outside and write like I used to. The book fell by the wayside and another failed project was on my resume. SMH.

~

As I look back over my life, I see a trail of failed projects, unfinished work, and terrible choices. It is enough to make me not want to even try again. However, I know I must continue because I am in great company. My list of failures doesn't mean stop. On the contrary, it empowers me to do even more. To fail even greater. To be disappointed 1,000 more times. Why? Because it shows that I am trying and that I won't ever stop trying to be better and bigger.

After you have defined success, you must be willing to plan, network, strategize, study, prepare, and work for it. Success is not the destination; it is the journey.

Before you even get started on that journey, I want you to know that whatever you defined success as, it is possible. That is the absolute truth. IT IS POSSIBLE! No matter your age, sex, height, race, or educational status, it is possible. No matter who believes in you, no matter where you were born, no matter how much money you have, it is possible. No matter who helped you, no matter who left you, no matter who stayed. None of that matters. All that matters is that you believe that it is possible.

When I hold workshops, typically in high schools or colleges, I have this test that I do. I ask everyone, "Who in here believes that they can make $30k a year?" Normally about seventy-five percent of the hands go up. I then ask, "Who in here believes that they can make $30k a month?" Now about twenty-five percent of the hands go up. Finally, I ask, "Who in here believes that they can make $30k a week?" Only five percent of the hands go up. I am always amazed at the difference in each question and the fact that people eliminate themselves based on what they believe they can accomplish. I always explain that there is no additional effort required to raise your hand on the different questions.

The same effort it takes to raise your hand for $30k a year is the same effort required for $30k a week. I say, "I did not ask you how you can make $30k a week, but simply do you believe that you can make $30k a week?" If you cannot even believe that you can make a certain amount of money or attain a certain level of success, then it will not happen for you. Yet time after time people eliminate themselves simply by not being able to believe. So other people are not even disqualifying them, they disqualify themselves. Believing should be the easiest part to achieve as it requires no evidence.

That's right I said, believing requires no evidence whatsoever. It simply requires a decision. That decision must be made first before you can go further in life.

The 5 S's of Success

We have talked a lot about failure so far, but I want to end by sharing The 5 S's of Success. Some people may have heard of these, but if you have not please take note as this will save you a lot of time. If you ask everyone you know, "Who wants to be successful?" Over 95 percent would say yes, I bet. Yet out of that 95 percent who say yes, many are not aware of the process to achieve success. That is the reason many people do not achieve the level of success they desire. So, here we will quickly take a look at these 5 S's.

Sacrifice: A loss or something you give up for the sake of something better. That is an excellent definition. Sacrifice is a word that we really do not like; however, success starts with sacrifice. We must give up something or somethings if we want to reach another level in life. There is no way around it. If you want something greater, you must be willing to give up the lesser things. Even if the lesser things are things that you really enjoy or love. The true display of sacrifice is to stop doing something that you love.

Separation: The state of moving or being moved apart. You will notice that none of these words are words that we love. They actually remind me of when I was a child and got sick and my mother would give me cod liver oil. A few people may remember that. It tasted so bad, but it actually helped me to feel better. The same can be said about this success process. The ingredients may taste bad, but they will help your life to be much better.

There will have to be a separation for you once you make a sacrifice. That separation may be from people, habits, a location, or all of the above. As you make sacrifices most times the separations will be evident. Sometimes people make it easy for you and begin to remove themselves from you. They don't like the direction you are going in and they just stop coming around, which is good. However, sometimes you will have to make that decision for them. If you fail to make the necessary separations you will find additional stress, delays, and frustrations in your success process. If you don't like to hurt people's feelings this may be a tough one for you. But no matter how tough it may be, you have to take that cod liver oil and the sooner the better.

Struggle: To make forceful or violent efforts to get free from restraints. Another unpleasant word. Where are the good words? So, you have sacrificed, separated yourself, and now you are struggling. The people who you separated yourself from are looking at you while laughing and saying, "You are doing all that for what?" You are beginning to even doubt yourself saying, "Am I doing the right thing? Am I crazy? What am I doing?" The struggle is real, very real. Remember I am trying to give you some wisdom so that when these things happen you are not surprised. Your comfort zone will try to pull you back into old habits, friends, and circumstances. This is where you have to forcefully and violently keep yourself out. Do not turn back.

Suffering: Pain, distress, and hardships. Now you are in too deep. You can't turn back. Oh, you thought after the struggle you were good? Not even close. Until you suffer for what you really want, you don't really want it. Real tears, real pain, real frustration. Sometimes no sleep, no money, no answers, no help, no ideas, no friends, no, no, no. This is the suffering. Out of 100 people who want success maybe one percent make it past this part. Ninety-nine percent stopped because of various reasons, but you must see this out until the end.

Success: The accomplishment of a purpose or idea. Success is failure, just wearing a suit. You endure the same process for both, but with one you feel a little better. Success is not the end either as it is never-ending. Yes, you may have succeeded in one area but now you must go through the whole process again for something else. Except now you are wiser and you have more endurance. You are stronger now as you have proven to yourself that you can do it. You must embrace the journey and the experiences you are having, and nourish the relationships you are building.

Love the failures and the successes the same because the person you are becoming will be better off for it.

Live. Learn. Serve. Inspire. Go Get It!

A Perspective... A Mindset... An Action Plan...

Chip Baker

"I learned to GIVE not because I have much but because I know exactly how it feels to have NOTHING."
—Author Unknown

I am humbled and honored to have the privilege to be a part of this masterpiece. I know that this will be in the hands of many and will go down as one of the greatest archives highlighting some amazing men. My intention is to give you my all, everything I've got, my A game because I want this to be an inspiration to many and make my family proud. I have taken the blessings that God has given me and strived to use them to be a blessing to others. I am a conduit.

#blessedtobeablessing #humbleandhungry #gogetit #AgameeffortproducesAgameresults

In this chapter, I would like to discuss the steps that are key to becoming suited for success. One must have the proper perspective, the proper mind-set, and the proper action plan.

Live

"You don't have to strive to conquer the world, you just have to strive to conquer yourself."
—David Chen

Each opportunity prepares you for your next opportunity.

When I was a young boy, I had a little league coach that was an exceptional man and a great role model. He was my elementary school principal and ended up being the superintendent of the school district in my hometown. His family was like my second family. He made a positive difference in the lives of many. He was one that I knew I wanted to grow to be just like as a man.

In high school and in college, I always strived to work hard and do things the right way. Unbeknownst to me, those things were noticed. As I was almost done with college, I started to apply for my first teaching and coaching job. I did not know that the principal at one of the schools I had applied to had done some college observation hours under my former little league coach.

The principal reached out to him to see what kind of person I was. My former coach told the principal that I was a great guy and that he should give me an opportunity. That is exactly what he did! He gave me an opportunity. I am sure there were more qualified people in the running than me since it was my first job.

I tell you this story to illustrate to you how important it is to live intentionally. It creates an effect that will benefit you and everyone that you are blessed to come in contact with. Because I had chosen to work hard and do right, it was noticed. I was given a big opportunity to be in a career that I dreamed of being in. Being a teacher and coach allows me the privilege of making a positive impact on the lives of many each day. It all started from me living a life where I strived to live, work hard, and do things right. That journey has allowed me to be a teacher and coach, the creator of *Chip Baker- The Success Chronicles*, an author, and it has placed me right here with you sharing my story in this amazing masterpiece. Each opportunity has prepared me and set me up for the next opportunity.

*"The best preparation for tomorrow is
to do your best today."*
—*David Gibson*

Sometimes when we are striving to live, we can get overwhelmed when we only focus on the big picture. I would like to share with you a practice that I use in my life daily. I use this daily because I feel that it helps me reach my optimal level of success. I call it "The S.H.G. Principle." I believe that if we focus on three things each day, we will reach our destination efficiently. The S stands for SHOW UP. Each day we must be present for whatever it is that we have signed up for in our lives (i.e., relationships, job, self-care). We must live in the moment and cherish the special moments we are blessed to have. Nothing is promised. Time is a limited and valuable commodity. H is for HAVE A GREAT ATTITUDE. Our attitude determines our altitude. The way we view things determines if we will have the outcomes we desire. It is all about our mindset and our perspective. I like to say that my blood type is "Be Positive" because I know that if I view things in a positive way, I will receive positive outcomes. The G is for GIVE YOUR ALL. Effort counts! When you give maximum effort, you receive maximum benefits. You get what you give, and input is equal to output.

Learn

Knowledge is the key that opens the door to your success.

To be your best at whatever it is you want to be great at there must be knowledge acquired. We all must go through the process of acquiring knowledge. We are all capable of having opportunities given to us or getting lucky, but if we do not continue to acquire knowledge, we will not be able to sustain the level of success we desire.

"Know what you know, know what you don't know, put people around you that can help you be better at what you don't know."
—Coach Robert Walker

This key advice was given to me before I took a major step in my career. It made me search within to win and create a process for me to gain knowledge. I had to self-audit based on the career path I had chosen to take. I first had to look at what I knew. I then reflected on what I felt I needed to learn to help me be successful in my career. From there, I created a list of things that I felt I was deficient in and found people, read books, and used technology to attain the needed knowledge. Google and YouTube are amazing tools!

Serve

*"What makes up a picture? The megapixels...
it's the small things that count!"*
—*Anthony J. Davis*

Effort counts!

When we make the effort to do the small things, we receive it back in abundance. When we give service, we get it in return even though we are not doing it to receive rewards or benefits from it. We get it back because people see that it comes from an honest and pure servant's heart. One small act of kindness can create an everlasting positive ripple effect. I started *Chip Baker- The Success Chronicles* about three years ago and from the very beginning the biggest supporters have been family and people that I have given service to. I am greatly appreciative that they feel I am worthy of having the same efforts, if not more, returned to me by the unwavering support they have given me. For that I am truly grateful. Effort counts!

Addition is great but multiplication is better.

In our early stages of education, we learned the four basic operations of math. It is imperative that we become very skilled at them because as we progress to each grade level, the level of complexity in which we use the operations gets higher. While completing complex problems, the success of each step determines if the problem will be worked correctly. If there is one simple mistake in an operation or an error on one step is made, then the entire math problem is wrong.

I use this example to illustrate addition and multiplication with people and the service that we give. By ourselves, we can serve and add value to our world. When we give service, reach out to people, and create relationships with like-minded and like-hearted individuals, we are able to multiply the value we add to others from our service. It is a simple concept, but we must have a servant's heart to be able to make the process of multiplication work. It helps our world become a better place.

Inspire

"Let your light so shine before men, that they may see your good works, and glorify your Father which is in heaven."—Matthew 5:16 (KJV)

It is no secret that my foundation is deeply rooted in my faith. I have been taught some amazing faith-based principles by my family that have helped me throughout my life. On top of that, I have been through some tough things where I have had to put those principles into action. This has given me my own firsthand experience with faith. As they say, "Mama nem" can teach you some things but we have to go out and experience on our own to develop what we believe.

Then we can take what we believe and use it to let our light shine. At times, we will have to refer back to our home training. We all have a special light within us that God has given us. It is up to us to tap into it, own it, and then share it to inspire others. It will help them be better. That is the process of sowing seeds. When we sow good seeds into good soil and nurture them, we reap the benefits of the harvest. A good reminder for me is the church song that says, "This lil light of mine, I'm gonna let it shine!" As I strive to give service that is one song that I sing to myself to keep me headed on the right path to give inspiration.

When you show up, have a great attitude, and give your all on a daily basis you inspire others by being an example of what making a positive difference looks like.

Resilience is inspiring.

Resilience is defined as the capacity to recover quickly from difficulties; toughness. Even though we are positive and work hard to let our light shine, tough things will happen to us. None of us are immune from going through tough things.

What we must learn to do is grow through our go through. As we are experiencing those tough things, we must find the lessons within that will make us better. There is a blessing in every lesson. We just have to figure out what the lesson is and grow from it. This will allow our light to shine brighter. It will allow us to go from a dull 40-watt bulb impact to a brightly illuminating 100-watt bulb impact.

Go Get It!

Change your mindset, change your life.

It's not the things that happen to us that make us better people, it is how we look at the things that happen to us that make us better. It is all about perspective. Perspective is key! When our mindset is in the correct place, correct actions will follow. Our mindset controls our thoughts. Our thoughts control our emotions. Our emotions reflect our behaviors. Our behaviors and actions determine our performance. When we change our mindset, we literally change our life.

"Champions do extra! It takes you from good to great, from ordinary to extraordinary."
—James Kerr (Legacy)

It takes extra effort each day to go from good to great or from ordinary to extraordinary. I have the humble and hungry mindset. I know that God has blessed me to be a blessing, so I am humble and grateful for the blessings. I am striving to be a blessing to others each day.

I am also hongry to achieve more and be the best version of myself. And yes, I know that I spelled hungry wrong. I wanted you to understand how hooongry I am to be great! I am an ordinary guy working hard to achieve some extraordinary things. hooongry!

Go get it!

No success or extraordinary things are handed to us. We must take intentional actions, in a step-by-step process, to achieve extraordinary things. The mentality of attacking our success will help us achieve things that we may not have even thought were possible. Things seem to fall into place when we are living intentionally. It also makes our days exciting because we are ready and willing to take on any challenges that may come our way.

> *"What would you do if you knew you could not fail?"*
> —Dr. Robert Schuller

In closing, I would like to share a secret with you. The secret is that you and only you can control the outcome of what you want your life to be. When we realize that we are actually in control of how well we excel, or not, it changes three things. It changes our perspective, our mindset, and how we approach things with our actions. If we can believe it, we can achieve it!

> *Where your focus goes your energy flows.*
> *Where your energy flows your focus goes.*

We must decide to focus on what is important to us and devote all of our energy towards that. Keep the main thing the main thing. When we decide to do that things fall in line and we organically eliminate distractions. I like to think of it as putting on the big headphones and creating noise cancellation. Everything in our life will become clear, we will have clarity, and we will enjoy the "music" of our life.

In this chapter, I have had the amazing opportunity to share some insight on what I feel it takes for one to be suited for success in life. When I began speaking to groups and pouring life into others, I told myself that I would only draw on things that I have experienced. By doing this, I feel that it brings out my authentic passion for making a difference because I strive to be a positive role model. I am far from perfect, but I am definitely striving to be the best that I can be. Living the life that I live and experiencing things, learning lessons along the way, serving others the most humble way I know how, striving to inspire those that I am blessed to cross paths with, and having a go get it mentality while matching that with go get it actions is my personal perspective, mindset, and action plan that I live by on a daily basis. My goal is to not just leave a legacy. My goal is to live a legacy each day in all that I do. My hope is that you will be able to use this to help you live a legacy in your life as well. God bless you on your path to becoming suited for your personal success.

Go get it!!!!!!

Calm in the Face of Crisis

Frank E. Brady

My grandfather is a very important figure in my life. He is the man that showed me how to be a man through his example. Growing up, I watched him treat my grandmother like a queen. He was and has always been a natural provider that took care of his family. I remember when I was younger, I was prone to getting sick often and my health was not that great. My grandfather was there, he was always there. I lived under his roof. My mother told me one time that my grandfather physically carried me to the hospital when I was younger and extremely sick. I can remember so many times when my grandfather was there for me. He is a man that has been there for so many people, his own family and beyond, throughout his life. Something I remember most is how he reacted in the face of difficulty every time a crisis would happen. He was always grounded in his thoughts and made logical decisions when difficult situations were happening. He didn't allow emotions to dictate his decision-making; he took action and stayed consistent at all times.

You see, I don't remember him ever falling apart when the circumstances were tough. I remember him standing strong through every crisis.

Crisis is and has been a constant factor in our family. Specifically, it has been responding to and dealing with crisis that has been present all my life. Crisis is defined as a time of intense difficulty, trouble, or danger.

In the year 2009, when I was a junior in college, my grandmother (God rest her soul) was killed tragically when she was struck by a car. She was a force of compassion and love, and she shared those traits with everyone she came across. She was my grandfather's queen, and my second mother. I witnessed how hard that loss hit our family as a whole, it was devastating.

While in the midst of grieving, I felt helpless. I felt like in some way, shape, or form, I should have been there to save her. I knew that there was nothing I could have done though; it was out of my control. During that time, I made a promise to myself that I would be there for my family, that I would step up further as a support system. I became that and more for my family in the coming years. I became the peacemaker. And like my grandfather,

I became a provider. I helped out financially in situations and stepped up to guide or make big decisions in the face of crisis.

In August of 2017, I was in the state of Florida for a conference. Every time I'm in Florida, I go to visit my family that is out there. At the end of the conference, I started to hear that a hurricane was coming. The hurricane's name was Irma. I went online and watched some clips of how Irma hit Puerto Rico and Barbuda and destroyed both islands. The news was billing this storm as one of the worst hurricanes of all time. At the time, my grandfather along with my mother and uncle were living together in Florida. I immediately came to the conclusion that my family had to evacuate their home. I called my grandfather and spoke to him about the storm. He was dead set on not leaving. I was scheduled to fly back to Connecticut two days from when I found out about Hurricane Irma.

I had a difficult choice to make. I could choose to keep my flight back to Connecticut or stay in Florida and help my family. I remembered the devastation that losing my grandmother caused our family and decided that I would stay and fight for my grandfather's safety. If you lost a loved one in the past and an opportunity came up for you to protect another loved one, would you take it? For me it was an automatic decision.

I decided to stay in South Florida through Hurricane Irma to ride out the storm and protect my family. Throughout that ordeal, I had to face many obstacles including my family itself and the battle against my own mind and emotions.

When I arrived at my grandfather's home, my first order of business was to go shopping for food and supplies. I traveled to the local Walmart and when I got there, the shelves were already empty, water was scarce, and almost all the ice was gone.

The cash register checkout lines were so long that they were stretching back to the middle of the store. I left and went home to talk to my family, specifically my grandfather, about evacuating the home. I stated to him that I had even spoken to the fire department about the availability of emergency rescue services during the storm. They stated that they could not come to any residence if winds were above 40 miles per hour because that is a safety issue for first responders.

We talked about all the possibilities, including the danger of staying and how vulnerable he was at his age (93), yet he refused. After the conversation, my grandfather received a call from the city emergency services with some important information.

They stated to him that because of his vulnerability, he was strongly urged to evacuate, which he agreed upon. While getting ready to leave, he was hit with a ministroke. I believe that was due to the stress and preparation regarding the storm. I had to think and act fast. I remembered that his neighbor was a nurse, so I went across the street and grabbed her to come evaluate my grandfather. She told me, "You need to call the ambulance now." The ambulance came and took my grandfather to the hospital. I proceeded to travel to the hospital as well to be with him and to get a handle on what was happening. Upon arriving at the hospital, I spoke with the doctor that was treating my grandfather.

While my grandfather was in the hospital, I was thinking to myself, "The hurricane is supposed to hit tomorrow morning. What do I do about my family and where they will be?" I then remembered a conversation I had earlier in the day with a man who told me that I could ask the hospital to keep my grandfather during the storm. So, I had that conversation with the head physician. I also got them to agree to allow my uncle to stay with my grandfather. That was one victory. I knew that at least my grandfather and uncle would be safe. I called my uncle and gave him the update. He packed his belongings and I called a rideshare service to pick him up and bring him to the hospital. The doctor told me that my grandfather was stable, and they were monitoring his vitals. I sat with my grandfather and watched him. His eyes were closed, and he was still. Tears started to well up in my eyes. In that moment, I promised myself that I would carry him through this situation as he carried me when I was young.

As I was leaving the hospital, I proceeded to search for hotels around the area where my mother and I could stay. They were all booked. After speaking with a man outside the waiting area, he directed me to some storm shelters around the area. I went home, spoke to my mother, and convinced her to come with me to stay at a local shelter. We left soon after. Over the next 48 hours, the storm raged through Florida as I sat with and took care of my mother. After the hurricane, we returned home to find out that a tree had been blown over and almost fell on the house. I immediately thought to myself, "It could have fallen on the house. And what if my grandfather had stayed and the shock had caused him to have a stroke while the storm was happening?" With winds over 40 miles per hour, would the first responders have been able to save him? Although we returned to a house without power, I was grateful it was intact. That same day, I called the hospital to check in on my grandfather and I called a rideshare service to bring my uncle home. For the next two weeks, I would travel to the hospital daily to check in on my grandfather, talk to doctors, and also keep my extended family across the country informed of what was happening.

While I was visiting my grandfather, I observed that his condition wasn't improving, and the doctors were ready to release him to a rehabilitation center. He wasn't able to walk on his own, his speech was slurred, and he would even have trouble keeping his eyes open. This wasn't the state my grandfather was in before; this wasn't his baseline health. I had a few conversations with the nursing staff and the head doctor about my grandfather's care. I explained to the head doctor in particular that he was about to be released from the hospital unable to walk. The doctor said that his walking again would not be guaranteed. Something in me would NOT accept that statement. I ended up reacting emotionally at first because the doctor was dismissing my claims and concerns.

I took a step back from the conversation and reminded myself to stay calm and grounded, and to analyze the situation for what it was. What were the facts? The main fact was that my grandfather was healthy before the ministroke but his baseline that the hospital was getting ready to send him out with was not healthy. I also realized that communicating with the doctor from a place of how bad I felt was not getting my point across to her.

I sat down. And during a moment of reflecting on the obstacles and problems I faced in the past, I remembered something important. As a resident advisor in college, I used to have to write detailed incident reports when I dealt with high-risk situations. So, I decided to write an incident report in the form of a letter and leave it for the doctor to read. I placed the letter in the doctor's mailbox, left the hospital that night, and went back to my grandfather's house. The next evening, I returned to the hospital to check in on my grandfather and to speak to the doctor again. When I spoke with the doctor, she told me she had read my letter and immediately ordered a neurological examination for my grandfather. The results came back that he was dealing with neurological issues due to the extreme stress likely brought on by the hurricane. The doctor and her staff were able to catch that early enough to prescribe him medicine. I was overjoyed, blessed, and so happy because through perseverance and staying grounded, my grandfather was going to make it through. The medicine coupled with rehab would help him get back to his baseline.

I left the hospital and two days later I flew back home to Connecticut. I was happy that my grandfather had made it and my family was safe.

My mother sent me a video of my grandfather walking on his own outside his house. I was overjoyed to see that; it brought tears to my eyes and gave me a sense of peace. At the age of 93 years old, my grandfather survived what could have taken him out.

I sat down and reflected on what I did to make it through that ordeal. I learned that the key was staying grounded no matter what. I didn't allow my emotions or the worst-case scenarios the doctor presented to make me fall apart.

I realized that I was ready to pursue the life of my dreams when I came out on the other side of that crisis. Since I was able to conquer and overcome that situation, I could apply the same process I used to other areas of my life.

It was all about controlling my thoughts, which led to me controlling my emotions and taking clear actions. In high-pressure crisis situations, the first piece of us that tends to be affected are our thoughts. We allow the negative ideas to replay in our minds and that breaks us down. We also allow what we think will happen to play over and over in our minds when nothing has even happened yet, but we give energy and power to those negative outcomes.

Have you ever replayed a negative thought in your mind?

That is something that can cause us to not be able to take action. I had no choice in that situation but to hold it together and stay strong, even when things looked dark. My mother, uncle, and many other family members from across the country were counting on me. Every time I walked into that hospital, I repeated my grandmother's favorite Scripture, "Ye though I walk through the valley of the shadow of death, I shall fear no evil, for thou art with me." That Scripture is what I used to relax my thoughts, alleviate my nervousness, and prepare me for whatever was about to happen.

I need you to lock in on this because this principle can save your life or the lives of your loved ones one day. It can cause you to avoid falling apart when there are big moments and situations at stake.

When crisis is happening, you may not be able to control what's happening around you, but you can control what's happening inside of you. When you control what's happening inside of you, you make better decisions that impact what's happening around you. During a crisis, never fold, stay grounded, and keep your thoughts clear.

I'd like to take you through an activity that I put together once I was able to reflect on what I went through.

You'll need a pen and a piece of paper. You also want to be in a quiet and peaceful place. Here are the instructions, take a moment and do the following:

1. Think of some of the difficult life experiences (crisis situations) you have had to overcome.

2. Write down as many that come to your mind as possible.

3. Choose one specific situation.

4. Answer the following questions: How did I get through that situation? What actions did I take? (Be as detailed as possible).

5. Once you've written down your actions, place them in order of what you did first to what you did last.

6. Take a few minutes to reflect on how the situation turned out.

7. This is where you ask yourself, "How did going through that situation impact me? Did it change me? What did I learn about myself?"

8. Once you've finished step 7, go back to step 5, look through the actions you've taken in the past, and see if any of those actions can be used to deal with a current obstacle or problem in your life.

9. Once you've answered these questions step by step, repeat steps 1-8 for different situations you have gone through.

The process you just went through allowed you to reflect on past challenges and problems. I also hope you were able to understand that what you've been through in your past can be used to help you deal with your present situations. We often have the opportunity to just sit and process what we've been through.

Life will challenge you; it will stretch you. But don't you fold. No matter what, you stand. As a man, you have to stand. As difficult as life is, as tough as crisis can be, remember that you control what's going on inside your mind; you control your actions. That control is the key to your success. That is the key to you overcoming crisis in your life.

The Revision: A Story of Success with Multiple Corrections and Attempts to Become Successful

Derek Cradle

The person you see today is a revised version from 1973. Growing up in White Plains, New York, during the rise of hip-hop, crack, and low academic expectations, I struggled to become the man you know today.

I was raised by a loving mother and stepfather, a grandmother who prayed endlessly, and a father who was figuring out how to father me from a distance. My family structure, my family economics, and my culture provided me with enough substance to navigate a complex system of traps, missed opportunities, functional and dysfunctional relationships, and everything else that might have led to no-to-low productivity or success. In all honesty, my spiritual life was my lifeline. To God be the glory. Calvary Baptist Church; Reverend Lester Cousins; my grandmother, Rosalie B. Grice

(Drumgold); my grandfather, Elijah Smalls; my great-aunt, Verdell Hilliard; and many other family members were and still are God-fearing folks. Their love for God was pasted into my life.

1973-1991: "Ain't No Stoppin' Us Now" by McFadden & Whitehead

A gray family house with a communal porch located at 14/16 South Kensico Avenue is where my parents birthed me. I remember calling this house the "broken" house, because it always seemed to be broken. I recall my mom always saying something about the house not being fixed or needing to be fixed. The family dog was the classic German Shepherd; his name was Shannon. My parents, both from low-income households, were high school sweethearts. They were raised in special neighborhoods of White Plains where African Americans either rented or eventually owned property (Brookfield Street, North Kensico, and the Windbrook Housing Projects). They attended Calvary Baptist Church and were well known in the community. Their marriage would birth two sons. I was born in 1973 and Keith the following year. William and Sheila would eventually divorce, and by 1977, I began to see life and recognize my talents.

Enrolled into the White Plains Public School system, I enjoyed school and loved to learn. By the second grade, I was tracked as a gifted and talented student; however, the transition to the gifted and talented program (M.A.S.P.- More Able Student Program) was not successful. The transition required me to learn with other students (a majority of white students) and work inorganically. In M.A.S.P., instruction was intense, the students were different, the environment was stifling, and I shut down within days. A meeting between my mother and teachers eventually returned me to general education. I was stained and hurt. I was confused. I would never be the same student. What I did realize was that I could coast and do just enough in school to earn a solid report card and still be social enough to be accepted by the classmates I loved. I was successful in elementary school. I missed a few assignments, but I did enough each year to be promoted.

By 1985, when I entered middle school, my love for hip-hop was steadily growing. My first album was *Down by Law* by MC Shan. That album trained my ears. Then it was Lord Finesse and his single, "Strictly for the Ladies," that had me open off drumbeats. Hip-hop during that era provided a compilation of artists and sounds that poured endless swag into my spirit. As the crack epidemic swept into New York City and the surrounding suburbs in the early to mid-eighties, the mix of hip hop and drug cultures was a confusing brew for me to swallow. I loved the music, the message, and all the materialism that came with these two societal elements. As a middle school student, I began to do fewer academic things and looked forward to the sweet smell and sounds of the streets. I wanted to be down!

1991-1999: "All for One" by Brand Nubian

I would eventually graduate from White Plains High School in June 1991. The truth was that we all graduated from White Plains High School. But the big question was, were we prepared academically for life after high school? I clearly was not. As previously mentioned, school had become tertiary to hip-hop and the drug culture. I was in love with the streets. As I was leaving high school graduation at the Westchester County Center, it dawned on me that life was changing, and I was not really sure what would be my next steps. During the spring of my senior year in high school, my mom had given me two choices—either I serve my country in the military or pursue higher education. Initially, the military seemed like the easiest and best choice. I submitted applications to a few HBCUs and entertained the Air Force. Recruitment officers were too persistent and helped me not to go down that path. Delaware State College (now Delaware State University) was the only college acceptance I received. By that time, my friends were everything and we spent each day together listening to hip hop, smoking blunts, drinking forty-ounce beers, sexing girls, playing basketball, selling crack, and waiting for new sneakers and gear to be released. That was the life.

In July of 1991, Delaware State College hosted freshmen orientation. That orientation was the beginning of my revision. By the end of that weekend, I was sold on life in Dover, Delaware. Not because I wanted to pursue a degree, but because a liquor store was right across the street from the campus, the grass of the yard was the greenest grass I had ever seen (it was amazing), there were no police to harass me, and the selection of females was mind blowing. At 18 years of age, Delaware State College was the newest playground for me, and I wanted it. Once committed to going to college in the fall of 1991, my mother assured her investment in me by sending me out to Amityville, Long Island, for three weeks prior to me leaving for school in August. She knew my flow and she knew my passions—hip hop, crack, and the streets of White Plains—would not be victorious.

During those three weeks I spent with my father, I learned of his struggles and missteps. My dad had fallen on hard times, but one thing about him was that he would figure out how to pull himself up time and time again. While I was in college, my father would write me letters of encouragement and share how proud he was of me. If only he'd known that the first two years of college were years of me re-tooling myself on how to read and write and struggling with Algebra. My freshmen year was all about getting to know the yard. It was about finding that balance and not losing myself to independence and newfound responsibilities. I survived and used my savviness to navigate those new waters. I would make several trips back home to White Plains, but one trip back home had me think deeply about my life.

On a Friday visit home from college in early October 1991, my friends were celebrating my homecoming, and one of them snatched a person's gold necklace. The rest of my friends were totally caught off guard by his actions, and we would eventually be interrogated by the police for a crime we did not commit. In that moment, I saw my newfound love of Delaware State College potentially slipping away and a new ride to Valhalla Correctional Facility as imminent. If I did not insist that I was a freshman in college, I might have never returned to college. From that experience, I learned the lesson that college was the place to be! Once my eyes were open, the college life was the life for me.

After two years at Del State, my focus was different. I embraced the college culture, made the Dean's List, and joined the fraternal organization, Omega Psi Phi, in 1994. Over the next five years, I excelled in school obtaining my undergraduate and master's degrees and landed my first teaching position in the Capital School District in Dover, Delaware. But I still needed some revision; I was partying, working, praying, and not clear on the next steps needed to move my life forward after college in Delaware. I decided to move back to White Plains and start over. I packed up a U-Haul truck and ended that era in September 1999.

1999-2019: "Life is Good" by Nas

I moved back home to recalibrate and find my focus. I dated a few ladies, and eventually I met my wife in 2001. I met her at an industry party at Club Bliss in Manhattan. She was with her sister and friends and I was with my people. We didn't date long; I was ready for a long-term relationship and so was she. On April 20, 2002, I married my pregnant girlfriend and on May 2, 2002, my first daughter was born. That was a very difficult time for me. I was learning how to be a husband and a father. I struggled. The marriage required compromise and clear communication. Those were things I needed to work on. In my fraternity, they instill the importance of manhood and family.

In late October 2002, my wife and I purchased our first home in Bed-Stuy. I directed all of my energy into my new marriage, new child, and new home. Even though I felt that time was difficult, I loved every moment of it. I was growing. I had made more revisions. My wife would have some difficult pregnancies and I would grieve in solitude. After teaching in White Plains, I took a leadership job in the Bronx, and finally accepted a teaching appointment as a New York City teacher. It was one of the best moves I made. I worked on my craft and returned to school to earn an advanced degree in school leadership. In 2006, the purchase of a second home in Maryland and traveling to Acapulco helped me to see the value of my family and friends. In 2008, my second daughter was added to our family and President Obama was elected. That election furthered my revision. The first

African American president was the coolest thing since hip-hop, drug culture, and Delaware State. I finally had a role model that I could use as an exemplar in real time. The next eight years would inspire me to lead my community, strive for higher positions in my career, embrace my wife and children differently, and struggle productively.

I have come to realize that life is mercurial, and revision is good. Through my reflections and experiences, each revision has led me to more success.

From Dunce to Doctorate: Mentoring Matters

Dr. Michael P. Rodriguez

I am Dr. Michael P. Rodriguez and I am not supposed to exist. Dr. Rod, as I'm called, should not be here. I have an earned doctorate degree, but I have a secret. I barely made it through high school. The personhood of Dr. Michael Rodriguez was never supposed to happen. I was not supposed to earn a high school diploma let alone a doctorate degree.

Hi IQ

The first IQ test I remember taking was late in the summer before sixth grade. That summer, my parents moved our family to a new state. To enroll in school, I had to take a test. I didn't know it was an IQ test. For me it was an entrance test for a new school, so I went in there and killed it! I thought, *Test done, now let me get back to enjoying this great weather and summer fun.*

My new school had ten sections of grades ranging from 6-1 to 6-10. Section 6-1 was for gifted and brainy kids who were being prepared to take over the world. Section 6-10 was for the kids who were intellectually challenged. They were older and needed supervision. I figured myself a smart guy, so I would definitely track for 6-2 maybe 6-3 if that evil thing called math got in the way of the school seeing my brilliance.

I was placed in section 6-9. Oh damn, hold up. What's going on here? I tested into section 6-9? I was confused. My ego was crushed. Worst of all, I was branded a 6-9 kid. From the moment I stepped into that 6-9 classroom, I was labeled as having an intellectual barrier that slowed my learning process. And like so many young people, I embraced the label. You think I am slow? I'll show you what that means. My behavior and attitude conformed to meet the preconceived expectations. I didn't study. I didn't do homework. I became a 6-9 kid. I allowed myself to believe the label. Us 6-9 kids knew what that meant and relished in it. We embraced the label and allowing others to define who we were.

Serve and Protect

I got through junior high and even managed to slide through high school. I was at the bottom of my class, but I counted it as a win because I finished. What would I do next? I had to do something with my life. So, like many others, I decided to join the military. I thought, *Hey, I get to see the world, make money, and do something positive with my life.*

I remember the morning the recruiter picked me up to take me to the Military Entrance Processing Station. As he pulled up, I walked out the door before he had gotten out of the car. He smiled and said, "Yeah, that's what I like to see. I don't even have to wait on you. Now that's how Marines do it." I grinned from ear to ear and thought, "I like the sound of that."

I was nervous but excited. I was about to change the course of my life. I would have purpose. I was going to serve. I was going to be a Marine.

Height measured, weight taken, sight, hearing, and a bunch of other tests completed, I sat and waited for my recruiter to tell me what was next. After a few minutes he showed up, stood flat footed, and as deadpan as he could he stated, "You failed the eye test. You can't be a Marine. Let's go."

I waited to see if he was joking but he stood there, glaring at me.

"What do you mean I failed? How did I fail an eye test? I'm wearing contacts. I got 20/20 vision with these things!"

He started to make his way to the car. I followed, full of hurt, confused, and crushed. My mind was spinning and then it happened. I heard it, faint at first, but then it became clear. It was the group of men and women that just tested with me being sworn in. I could feel my emotions swelling up inside. I breathed deeply and spoke to myself, "Relax, Mike." I took a few more deep breaths. It wasn't working. I felt the tears forming.

I held it together until we reached the car. But as I lowered myself into the car, I wasn't just sitting, I was sinking. Slowly descending into hopelessness. My future just came to an end. I had nothing left, I was nothing. Tears began to fall. He drove in silence. I cried in silence. I was replete with hurt. I felt bloated and overstuffed from what seemed like a lifetime of disappointment. Forget dreams, I would live day to day because that's what 6-9 kids do.

I'll House You

Over the following months, I connected with a group of guys from the neighborhood. We had one thing in common, we loved to go clubbing. Give us music, drinks, and a room full of girls and we were happy. We developed a routine. We worked part-time jobs, collected checks, and partied every weekend. We had a Thursday, Friday, Sunday, and even a Tuesday nightspot. But Saturday night was the highlight. It didn't matter what we did that week, we had to make it to the Saturday nightspot.

I had a myriad of jobs. I worked at a jewelry factory, mailing facility, and retail stores. I even worked as a garbage man one summer. Mostly, I worked at fast food restaurants. Too many to recall. To sum up my work experience, I flipped burgers and stuffed tacos. There is nothing wrong with flipping burgers or stuffing tacos for a living, but for me it was just something to do.

There is freedom in aimlessness. Living without the weight of expectation allowed me to live in the moment. I wasn't concerned with the future. The day was what mattered. What me and my dudes were doing, where we were hanging out, who we were going to see, and how much fun we were going to have at the club was what mattered. I could see it—the flashing lights and beautiful bodies swaying in rhythm. The smiling faces as eyes met on the dance floor. I could hear it—the bass pounding out beats that transported me far away. The rhythmic clapping that occurs when everyone's favorite house song plays. The only thing that mattered was the music and the moment.

Me and the crew partied and played. We laughed, shouted, pontificated about current events, and challenged each other with our wit and wisdom. We bonded like brothers. Our common experiences became our epoxy and we just lived. We dreamed a little, we planned a little, but mostly we just lived without expectation. Then I ran into Lee.

Lee and Me

Lee lived on my block. I've known him since junior high school. We went to the same schools, but Lee was not a 6-9 kid. He was a 6-2 kid—smart and a nerd. He was always cool to me but that might have been because I knew him. I knew who he really was. If you didn't know him, you quickly noticed the hard-top black dress shoes he liked to wear with khakis, a button-up shirt, and the huge calculator watch he sported on his wrist. When he spoke, you heard his high-pitched nasal voice that raised higher when he got excited, which was often. I hadn't seen Lee in a while, so I was pleased to see him.

"Hey, Lee, what's going on? I haven't seen you in a while. Maybe since graduation, right?" Lee walked up and raised his hand to give me a hand-shake and pull me in for a one-armed half-hug, but he missed my hand and we awkwardly greeted with a loose handshake and a pat on the shoulder.

"Hey, Mike, good to see you. I am doing great!" I could hear his excitement building as he spoke.

"I just finished college..." he started. My mind froze and I thought, *Wait, isn't college four years? He said he finished college. It's been four years since high school? I went numb. Did four years really pass that quickly?*

Lee continued, "I've been doing an internship I got through my uncle. Well, he's not really my uncle, I just call him that. I think he's messing with my mom, but since my dad died it's okay cause he did get me this really great internship."

Lee's lips were moving a mile a minute. "Through the internship I secured a job on Wall Street. Yeah, that Wall Street. Mike, I'm going to be making $80,000 a year. This is fantastic, life is great!" he shouted. He then looked at me full of excitement and expectation and spoke six words that shot through my soul, "What have you been up to?"

I stood there glaring at Lee. Frozen in the moment. Standing in front of Lee I saw for the first time who I had become. Dressed in my fast food uniform, shirt stained with taco sauce, dried lettuce, and Grade-D beef, I thought, *What have I been up to?* Looking at my life in juxtaposition to Lee's, nothing of relevance came to mind. The clubs, the minimum wage jobs, and the hours of pontificating about world events, laughing at empty jokes, and contemplating life seemed meaningless. What had I done with my life these past four years? I was wearing the sum of the past four years on a stained t-shirt. That was what I had to show. I was a 6-9 kid so what could I expect?

But me and Lee are from the same block. He might have been smarter in the classroom, but we stood there eye to eye on the same concrete and he was expecting a similar story from me. He saw no difference between us. He saw no difference between a 6-2 kid and 6-9 kid because we lived on the same block. He knew who I was. He didn't see me as a 6-9 kid, only I did. I realized that my belief that I was a 6-9 kid was still with me and I had allowed that false belief to define me, to control my actions, and to determine who I became. I hadn't been labeled a 6-9 kid since sixth grade, but I had been labeling myself a 6-9 kid for the past ten years.

Being labeled is often not the worst thing that can happen, especially when we realize that we have all been labeled. We carry labels from our parents or other family members and friends. Positive labels build up our self-esteem and give us the confidence to try new things. But it's those negative labels that seem to adhere to our ego with the greatest of ease.

Speak to your average adult and they can recall a moment in grade school or junior high when someone called them a name. That adult can replay the incident as if it just happened that day. Not only can they describe the event in detail, but with emotional impact as well. We carry emotional hurt for years. Negative labels create negative emotions that wound our self-worth and damage our dreams causing us not to believe in ourselves. Being labeled happens to all of us, but the problem occurs when we accept the label as truth. We internalize the label and make it part of who we are.

I believed the label. I believed the lie. I lived the lie.

But at that moment standing before Lee, something changed. I saw myself as who he saw me to be, a regular kid from the block who had all the potential he was demonstrating. In that millisecond, I decided to no longer be a 6-9 kid. I didn't know who I would become, but I would no longer personify a 6-9 kid.

I encourage you to throw off the labels you've carried. Someone may have called you dumb or stupid, they may have told you that you would never amount to anything, they may have said you would be a nobody, but I challenge you today to shake off those labels and begin to walk in your own greatness.

But your question may be, "How do I do that?"

Change Your Personal Soundtrack

First, change your personal soundtrack. We all have a personal soundtrack. An amalgamation of the voices in our head. Your soundtrack can be made up of the voices of your parents or grandparents, a teacher, or a friend. The music we listen to and the television shows we watch also become a part of our personal soundtrack. They are the voices that direct us as we go along our life's journey. We hear these voices over and over and they become part of our self-talk which echoes what we think of ourselves. In my case, "You're a 6-9 kid" became "I'm a 6-9 kid." "You're slow" became "I am slow." I personalized the message. And like me, so many of us personalize negative messages.

To change your personal soundtrack, change who and what you listen to. Find positive messages to listen to daily. There are many motivational and uplifting messages, and positive sounds and shows available at our fingertips. Let them become a part of your daily intake and get yourself a personal mantra. Mine is simple, "Be bold, be strong, be amazing, be you." Find words to tell yourself, "I am awesome, happy, intelligent, great." If you can't think of anything to say, use my mantra, "Be bold, be strong, be amazing, be you!" Rehearse it daily until it becomes your new soundtrack.

Find a Mentor

Find someone who can mentor you. You may be wondering, "How do I find a mentor?" Start by asking those close to you. It can be a teacher, relative, or a close family friend. Speak to someone who is doing something you are interested in and ask them to help guide you.

Lee became my first mentor and he was one of many. At the time, I didn't even know he was mentoring me. We met a few times after we reconnected, and he told me his path to the internship. We talked about what college was like and what his next steps would be. I listened, I learned, I was inspired. I told him what I thought I might want to do with my life. We discussed what skills I thought I had and through it all, he listened. His belief in me didn't waiver. Soon after, he left to do his internship and secured a job on Wall Street.

I eventually followed my own path, meeting many more Lee's throughout my life. I am grateful for the mentors I've had along the way. I am not at the end of my journey, but I've progressed so much from where I started.

I am Dr. Michael P. Rodriguez. I exist. I am here. I am a mentor.

Listen Carefully, Your Purpose Knows the Way

Gerald Yarborough

Today, I have the privilege of getting paid to do what I love while making an impact. A career in art can be a parent's worst nightmare, but I beat the odds and followed my dreams despite the clear obstacles. Art in return saved my life. Today, I get the opportunity to help others see that you can be successful in the competitive entertainment field. The look on a young artist's face when they realize that if I did it they can do it too is the most rewarding part of my career, because I remember what the other side felt like.

Growing up in Jamaica, Queens, as the middle child in a family of five was interesting. My father was a retired MTA worker who did photography on the side and my mother was a special education teacher. In a way, I was always trying to find my identity in the world. I just liked to draw and paint, but it felt like I was living in my brother's shadow.

The other choice at the time was the streets with my friend, but that path never looked like it led anywhere. My dad had a suggestion for what I should do to be successful and get out of the hood. He told me to be a doctor or lawyer. That was the goal growing up as an African American male in Queens. He would often say, "Artists don't make no money. You need a safe, good job with a pension." You see, my dad learned that tough lesson from experience. Once an accomplished musician in his own right, who at a time played with legends like Duke Ellington, he was forced to give up the unstable life of an artist for stability. He drove a bus for 25 years and worked a number of side hustles to provide for his family. I can honestly say that when I was younger, I didn't realize or appreciate his sacrifice. But I came to understand the full magnitude of his sacrifice when I got older. In fact, today I think I used his fear of me falling into the same trap as motivation to dream beyond what life allowed him to see.

The Day It All Changed

My dream of art quickly took a back burner during my teenage years. I'm not sure if I allowed my dad's fears of being a starving artist or just my desire for money and what I saw as success to change my heart, but money and job stability became my motivations over my passion. I was excelling in my studies in pre-med, and art at that point was just a hobby to get attention. That choice would prove to be unfulfilling in the long run.

A wise man once told me, "You cannot split your A.T.O.M. (Ability, Time, Opportunity, and Money)." Atoms make up everything around us. In science class, I learned that when you split an atom there is complete chaos which often concludes with an explosion that destroys everything around it. The same can be said about our lives. Your God-given gift or ability requires time for you to perfect it, which prepares you for an opportunity to use that gift to build wealth. When you try to split these important factors in your life, it only ends in destruction and frustration. I was running from my purpose and true love chasing someone else's dream, but that would soon change with one life-altering event and an uncomfortable conversation with my biggest fan.

It was a cold Sunday afternoon in December, four days after Christmas. I was on punishment for fighting with my dad, and a number of horrible choices you make at sixteen. As book smart as I was, I always found myself in some drama. I remember that day so vividly. I was sitting on the edge of my mother's bed and she said, "Out of all my kids, you are the only one who disappoints me. You have so much potential and you are going to blow it with your friends. Follow your dreams. Don't waste your gifts. Don't screw up." Those were among the last words my mother said to me before she left. She went to the hospital that night for a simple blood transfusion and six hours later we got a phone call saying that she passed away. That was one of the worst conversations you could have with your mother before losing her forever. All I could think of was how much I disappointed her because I was wasting my potential. When I looked into her eyes and heard those words, it literally broke my heart. I knew I had to do something; I had to change. I missed my mother and there was no better way to honor her memory than to do the right thing. I decided to put my passion first and stop wasting time running from my calling. My only fear was that it might be too late because my scholarship for pharmacy at Saint John's University was already secured. Her words have been my motivation throughout my adult life.

It was late 1998 and I was a freshman at St. John's University, settling into my studies as a pharmacy major. I had everything lined up—a five-year scholarship with the hopes of a good paying job in a high demand field likely upon graduation. Yet, I was haunted by my mother's persistent directive. The truth is I was not following my dreams. I was not living my purpose.

That feeling grew stronger every day and I knew pharmaceuticals just wasn't for me. I felt as though I was wasting my true gift: art. So, I focused my full attention on my art electives. But after one year, St. John's warned me that if I didn't start taking sciences courses, I would lose my scholarship. I soon did and I was devastated. The entire time, my mother's simple proclamation ate at me. Uncertain about what to do, I chose to drop out of school instead of falling into debt with student loans. I told myself that if art was the path and my true purpose in life, God would make a way. So, at that time, it appeared that school was no longer in God's plan for me. Therefore, my dad who worked all of his life said to me, "If a man doesn't work, he doesn't eat." So, I got a job working in customer service at Geico Direct.

I was not looking forward to that change in my life, but I felt that at least I could make enough money to get a car or something. So, I reluctantly took the job. That was how far I could see that job opportunity taking me. But little did I know, God had so much more in store for me. On my very first day at Geico, I met a young woman and I could not take my eyes off of her. She sat down across from me and we had a long conversation. Or, more like I told her my life story and she listened. I knew right then and there that she was my wife. In fact, moments after meeting her, I spoke it out loud to one of my friends who got me the job. He laughed at me, but wouldn't you know that the same special woman would later become my wife. So, what had seemed like a detour from my purpose had turned out to be a central piece of His larger life plan. But other things weren't so certain because after a massive car accident that summer, I was left on disability and in rehab for months. That caused me to wonder if I had screwed up by leaving school and was my dream of being a working artist ever going to happen? For months I was in heavy depression, but I had faith that it would all work out.

My Time, My Chance

Then one day when I was at my lowest, St. John's called. The funny thing was that they had been calling me for some time, but I'd been avoiding their calls because I thought I still owed money to the school after I dropped out. When I finally answered the call, to my surprise, it turned out to be great news in the form of another scholarship for me. This time, it was for art focusing on graphic design and advertising. Another student had dropped out and they wanted me to come back to make sure I didn't waste my talent. What should I do? Exactly what my mother told me to. I wanted to do art, and here was the opportunity I was waiting for. I always look at that time in my life as a pivotal moment. Was I in shock? Yes. Did I grow tremendously in faith and character through that time of uncertainty? Of course I did. It taught me the important lesson that there are no straight paths to what you want in life. But more importantly, it taught me that timing is everything. If I did not drop out when I did, I would have never met the love of my life or been in the position for that second chance at an art scholarship.

In life, some opportunities have a time stamp and you have to be prepared to work harder than anyone else to take advantage of those rare opportunities. I knew that for sure. So, I worked nights on the phones at Geico Direct and took an aggressive back-to-back twenty-one credit class load. It was a punishing schedule that I attributed to helping me learn the valuable project and time management skills that I use today. I could feel things beginning to turn around and in my last semester came the opportunity of a lifetime, an internship at Nickelodeon. My brother, who at the time was a senior designer at MTV, gave me a referral and said the same thing most family members say when they put their name on the line for you, "Don't mess this up." Sounds familiar, huh?

When I walked into the office for the first time, I was wearing my baggy jeans and I had my gold chain on. I was like, "Yeah, bring your whole self to work. This is going to be great!" I quickly figured out that wasn't going to work and I needed to dress for where I wanted to go. Even though I was only making copies, I saw myself as a creative director one day. So, I made up my mind to dress the part before the position came. Every day, I showed up in a suit and tie to make copies for the designers to send off to the show creators in Los Angeles. I did that for three months and let me just say I left a huge impression on the department because of how seriously I took my job.

When my internship was up, they didn't want to go back to making their own copies. I was hoping that I could get a job, but that seemed impossible due to budget cuts. There was a hiring freeze and rumors of possible layoffs on the horizon. I remember being so worried about my future on my last ride into the city that I went to the Bible for comfort. I turned to Matthew 6:30-31 (NIV) which says, "If that is how God clothes the grass of the field, which is here today and tomorrow is thrown into the fire, will he not much more clothe you—you of little faith? So do not worry." As soon as I got to work, I sat down, then the phone rang. It was my creative director, Tim Blankley. He asked me to come to his office. I said to myself, "This is it; the ride is over." I sat down in his office and he began to say how great it was to have me on the team and how much my presence would be missed. I thanked him for the opportunity, but he stopped me before I could say another word. He said, "What if we created a position for you?" I was like, "Huh?!" He explained that the designers were in an uproar about me leaving and begged for me to be made into a design assistant. That was a first for the department; unprecedented. I accepted and that is how my career at Nickelodeon started. I am a living witness that your gift will make room for you.

Preparation Meets Opportunity

My first big break at Nickelodeon came when Russell Simmons walked into our office. At the time, he owned Simmons Jewelry Co. and his team was trying to figure out how they could make high-end SpongeBob jewelry. I was invited to the meeting by my supervisor at the time with our creative director. I remember Russell being very upset with the design concepts the team showed them and saying that they were wack and we had no clue about urban jewelry. That was my chance. I knew that he was coming to the office, so the night before I worked on some designs of my own which I strategically placed on the table while he was ranting, making sure they caught his eye. I remember him looking down at them and saying, "These are hot." Then he turned to my supervisor and said, "Can big man work on this project?" At first, he was apprehensive, but Russell insisted. That opened up the opportunity for me to design my first major project and one of the most expensive pieces of jewelry in my career. It was a 12.8 carat yellow diamond pendant appraised at $75,000. It garnered awards and celebrity press from the Sundance Film Festival to the charity auction where it raised $250,000 to help save the oceans. I finally did it. But I could not celebrate too long because the work kept coming. After I proved myself on the Simmons Jewelry project, I tackled packaged goods by collaborating with companies like Colgate, Kellogg's, Kraft, and Good Humor on groundbreaking campaigns that pushed the envelope creatively and broke barriers in the kid's licensing world. All my hard work started to get me noticed by company stakeholders and paid off in promotions and opportunities to grow my personal brand of creative excellence. I quickly attached myself to some great mentors. They gravitated towards the excellence in me and my career flourished.

That new platform also birthed my passion for corporate social responsibility and mentorship. I was in a position to give back and help make the road for people of color who desire a career in art and entertainment a little easier. Teaching, especially young black men, the importance of showing up in your work and *being small enough to be digested, but big enough to be remembered*. I love hands-on mentorship because it has a lasting impact on the community. Currently, I serve on the boards of non-profits that work to close the gap on disparities plaguing underserved groups while building diversity and inclusion in media for organizations like Reel Works, Children's Health Fund, and New York Edge (formerly known as SASF, Sports and Arts in School Foundation); the largest provider of school-based, after-school services in New York City. SASF works with over 25,000 students in 150 schools across all five boroughs.

My most fulfilling work is prison outreach. Outside of my creative career, I am an ordained outreach pastor at St. Albans Gospel Assembly in Queens where I oversee our programs at Nassau

Correctional Facility in Long Island, New York. There I speak to inmates every month and have helped many of them find purpose in their lives over the past 14 years. My message to the inmates is, "The choices you make shape your life." I offer an invitation to change and provide a connection to a web of housing, jobs, churches, and legal and government contacts to help them do exactly that. The sad thing about it is that it's mostly young minority men that I get to mentor. When you lose young men from a neighborhood, you lose leaders, fathers, brothers, and a generation because nobody is left to train them on how to live right. So, I look forward to every interaction with them because it gives me an opportunity to change the neighborhoods I grew up in one man at a time.

Today, in my current role at Viacom Nickelodeon Consumer Products, I am the senior creative lead on the Global Creative Group where I played a pivotal role in growing the home goods category to generate $14.5 million in revenue through strategic partnership building and innovative design direction. I am responsible for managing and developing the design direction of all retail programs across not only Nickelodeon brands, but now BET, Comedy Central, MTV, and the Paramount portfolio.

How to Overcome a Toxic Environment

H. Ato-Bakari Chase

E em Htp. I greet you in peace and satisfaction. My name is Hubert Ato-Bakari Chase Jr. In fact, my full name is Medjhuty Ra En Ma'at Hubert Ato-Bakari Chase Jr. It may be a very long name, but it denotes my evolution as a man, a husband, and a father. My name punctuates my spiritual transformation and represents different stages of my life. Now, the purpose of this chapter is to provide a guide for you. This is intended for young men, especially teens and young adults of African descent. When I say of African descent, I am referring to black people primarily. Hopefully, this story will help guide and direct you on your journey to manhood and will provide insight into overcoming some of the challenges you will face along the way. My purpose for writing this is to show how I overcame a toxic environment and to say that you can too.

Now, when I say toxic, I'm referring to an environment that has the negative influences of gangs, guns, drugs, poverty, and violence as a normal part of life. Urban neighborhoods that are polluted with the type of energy and vibration that keeps one on edge. Before I go any further, it is critical, regardless of circumstance, that the person who wishes to escape such an environment is committed to doing so.

My Story: I was born in Georgetown, Guyana. My mom delivered me early on a Wednesday morning. In Guyana, we call this time of day "fore day mornin." These are the hours between 3:00 a.m. and 5:00 a.m., before the sun rises or before the day begins. Before I was born, everybody assumed I would be a girl. The reason was due to the fact that I was coming exactly 11 months and 22 days after my brother, Ru. My oldest brother and only sister are also "Irish twins" born 10 months apart. So, with my birth being so close to my brother's, the thought was that I would also be a girl. Nope! When the midwife pulled me out and saw my male appendages she exclaimed, "Oh another nigger man!"

The statement was made jokingly, but it was still profound on many levels. It is probably why I am driven to be an agent of change for those young men who may be in similar situations to mine. Also, it confirmed what my favorite emcee, Rakim, wrote in a verse of "The Ghetto" when he said:

"...Thinking how hard it was to be born,

Me being cream with no physical form...

Nine months later a job well done,

Make way, cuz hear I come..."

Yes, I was the champion who won my race against millions. If I didn't win, my parents very well could have had another daughter and my siblings could have had another sister. But I won, so I am here today after a job well done.

Fast forward to East Orange, New Jersey, a small city bordering Newark, New Jersey. In fact, I grew up literally on the border of Newark's Vailsburg section which we call Hoodaville. My house was one block in from South Orange Avenue. My childhood was spent at Boylan Street Recreation Center where I learned to swim, play ping pong, and shoot pool. I played youth basketball at the rec. I also played Pop Warner football in Vailsburg Park a few blocks away as well as in Elmwood Park in East Orange. I would often go to Alexander Street Library which was closer to my house than the Elmwood Branch Library in East Orange. You see, even though my address said East Orange, I was using the resources of my neighborhood which included Newark. That was important for me because it helped shaped me into the man I am today. It also provided the challenges I would overcome on the road to success.

I was raised by my mother (a divorced widow) and my aunt, Sheila, who sponsored my family's migration to the United States. As the youngest of six children, I received plenty of guidance from my older siblings. But, with the absence of a father whom I never knew, I could have gotten into all sorts of negative behaviors. I didn't know my father because my mother left him for good when I was three and he died when I was seven. He was a very abusive man and she could not take any more. That was a brave choice for my mother to make and I am very proud of her for doing it. It must have been a very hard decision. I watched my mother work odd jobs and put herself through an adult education program to finish school. Then, she secured a job working as a secretary which brought her and us some stability.

One of the fortunate things I benefitted from early on was the opportunity to play sports. My mother, to her credit, allowed all of her children to pursue their dreams. Football became my outlet and sports in general gave me a platform to be as aggressive as I wanted to be. It allowed little boys like me an opportunity to release our emotions, especially anger, in a constructive manner. I began playing football at the age of nine and continued throughout college. By age twelve, I was also playing basketball. I enjoyed basketball, but mainly played to stay in shape for football. As you see, I gravitated towards the team sports. I even tried baseball in the sixth grade. But that didn't work out, so I stuck with the other two. Sports provided me an opportunity to learn how to deal with adversity, how to persevere, and how to work on a team. It also allowed me the opportunity to stay away from negative behaviors or running the streets.

In addition to playing sports, I got involved in music. I began playing the drums in elementary school. By the time I got to middle school, I was the lead drummer in the band because I was the only one who could play the drum set. Another outlet was playing drums for the youth choir at church. My mother was a staunch Seventh Day Adventist Christian and she maintained that we go to church every Saturday. I played the drums at church for the youth choir, but I also went on small tours playing drums for gospel choirs and singers along the east coast. I got a chance to travel to different towns outside of East Orange and New Jersey and it was a tremendous gift.

Lastly, I got involved with civic groups, namely the Boy Scouts with Troop 8 (one of the oldest black troops in the country) and a mentoring program called City Life. I got into both of those programs following behind my older brother, Ru. He being roughly a year older than I, it was natural to follow him. Luckily, he led me into positive activities like these two which kept me busy and productive. In fact, there were times when I would be out of the house every night of the week, but I was involved in some activity. My mother knew where I was; she didn't have to worry about me running the streets.

As a result of participating in those activities, I kept my grades up in school. I only worked hard enough so that I could still play sports. It wasn't that I was a dummy. In fact, there wasn't a subject outside of math that I couldn't dominate. However, growing up in an urban environment, boys don't get points for being on the honor roll. They are rewarded for being able to play sports, being able to fight, having flashy clothes and jewelry, or any combination of those three. For me, sports and music were my avenues. So, I didn't get into too much trouble at school and I maintained my grades. Eventually as a senior at Newark Tech High School, I decided I wanted to go to college. Even though I played football, I never thought of going to college. I wanted to go to the NFL, as most kids do, but I knew in the back of my mind it was a pipe dream.

Even though I had a 2.4 GPA and a 740 SAT score, I was able to enter William Paterson College (now William Paterson University) under the Educational Opportunity Fund. EOF was created for low income, educationally disadvantaged students like me. William Paterson is located in Wayne, New Jersey, about an hour away from East Orange. It is a gated campus community which means that all of the campus is located on its own property. It is not in a city nor does it share buildings with other businesses. The campus was quiet and secluded with all kinds of animals I had only seen on TV like deer, rabbits, ground hogs, skunks, beavers, foxes, geese, and ducks. So, it was a very different environment and it caused me to almost drop out of college… the first time.

You see, I entered Willie P in August for football camp and I didn't return home until Thanksgiving. That was a long time even though I was only an hour away. I didn't have a car to go home or money for the bus. Plus, every weekend was a football game. So, when Thanksgiving break came, I packed my bags and headed home. As soon as I got home, I didn't even unpack. I went right back out the door, walked down to South Orange Avenue, hopped on the #31 bus, and headed to downtown Newark. Ahh! That's more like it. Within minutes, I heard the sirens of police cars and ambulances. I saw people hanging out on the corners and saw the dilapidated buildings and open lots with garbage strewn about. I heard people talking or arguing loudly and saw broken glass on the streets. Ahh! *This is home. This is me. This is where I belong.* Or so I thought. I didn't want to go back to William Paterson. I was experiencing home sickness and something even worse.

I was experiencing what I later understood was a concept called cognitive dissonance. Even though I was raised in a loving home, had coaches and mentors, and was involved in constructive activities, I was still negatively influenced by my environment. I felt like a fish out of water at William Paterson. The tranquility and calm surroundings were almost too much to take and almost drove me to quit college.

Cognitive dissonance is when you encounter a sharp or pronounced difference from whatever you are accustomed to. You experience something so new and different that it creates disharmony within you. If you don't push through and overcome it, cognitive dissonance may force you to return to old habits that are not in your best interest. For example, if Tyrone who constantly hears that he is bad has someone tell him he's good, he might go out and do something bad to prove to the person that he is in fact bad. Because he's accustomed to hearing negative comments about himself, the minute he hears something positive, it may cause discomfort; and, as if by reflex, he does something to bring about the negative comments. He has learned to function within that view of himself and believes that is who he is.

Dr. Carter G. Woodson, in *The Mis-Education of the Negro*, expressed this in a much more profound way when discussing the impact of a poor education. He said,

"When you control a man's thinking you don't have to worry about his actions... You don't have to tell him to go to the back door. In fact, if there is no back door, he will cut one for his special benefit. His education makes it necessary."

Dr. Woodson, if you don't know, is the founder of Black History Month. In his book, he explains how cognitive dissonance has worked on the minds of black people who have been told repeatedly that they have contributed nothing to human history and that they were only slaves. The fact that they continue to hear this false narrative creates dissonance, so much so that the person who believes it

H. Ato-Bakari Chase

will put himself last (the back door) even when it's not necessary for him to do so.

However, the beauty and the power of the human mind is that it can be transformed. It has the power to shift its paradigm. The human mind is a marvel.

I made the difficult decision to return to William Paterson. I didn't realize how impacted I was by my environment and how much I wanted to stay and be a part of it. Going back to Willie P was a wise decision. Eventually, I overcame my anxiety and grew to love the atmosphere. I realized that the change in scenery was very good for me and it helped me grow tremendously. I also realized that getting out of my environment gave me a different perspective. Ultimately, it provided the foundation for my work as an agent of change in that same environment. You see, I do not wish to teach, lead, or uplift youth in affluent or stable neighborhoods. Today, I work in the same environment that produced me so that I can help transform those who come after me.

I was able to transform my mind because I was able to trust the process. William Paterson allowed me to grow and develop. At the same time, it allowed me to see that I could return to my

84

environment and help to uplift it, not merely be comfortable in it.

So, to summarize, how do you overcome a toxic environment? First, take advantage of every opportunity you receive. I was very busy in my youth because I seized opportunities. Whether it was sports, music, civic groups, or mentoring programs, I seized the opportunities to participate, learn, and grow.

Secondly, don't be afraid to leave the nest. Even though I was filled with anxiety when I went to college, I wasn't initially afraid to go. Sometimes, we psych ourselves out and don't give ourselves a chance at something because we may be afraid to try it or to leave others behind. You will have to venture out on your own and you will be stronger for it.

Third, I continued to evolve. I did not stay stuck in the perception of who thought I was, a boy from the hood. I allowed myself to grow, to learn, and to evolve. This is the key to overcoming cognitive dissonance and to overcoming a toxic environment. I came into what is called knowledge of self. The knowledge and understanding of who I am as a human being of African descent whose ancestors established the first civilizations and all that goes with it. I learned the knowledge of my ancestors and my history. I also grew spiritually which is why I have such a long name.

Lastly, I had a moral and spiritual upbringing that did more than teach me about religion. It provided character development and discipline. It is important to have some form of spiritual foundation to get you through your tough times and to help you stay on course. It doesn't matter which religious doctrine you follow. Understanding that you are a part of a larger continuum of life and learning to submit to that great force is essential.

One more thing. I would be remiss if I didn't mention that I was fortunate to have older guys from my neighborhood who shielded me from the street life. They knew enough to do their "business" away from view and to push the younger ones away. These brothers, many of whom would pay a heavy price for their lifestyle, where thoughtful enough to keep me away from such a fate and I'm indebted to them because of it.

In conclusion, I hope this story has provided you with insight, ideas, and inspiration. I hope it helps you on your road to success and I wish you discover all that you dream of and more.

Shem em Htp. I leave you in peace and satisfaction.

I Was a 30-Year-Old Boy!

William Hodges

While writing this chapter, I struggled with transparency. What would I tell or how much would I reveal? Would I discuss my bad habits and illegal activities? Could I be honest about my lack of maturity? Would I share that I was content in my comfort zone, staying in the lane I was in, until there was inevitable construction on the road? Did I want my wife, daughter, family, and friends to know of my personal struggles? Did I want my daughter to know the issues I'd experienced raising her? Did I want to show my inadequacies, failures, and shortcomings? Would I speak on my fear of failure which was really fear of success? Yes, I wanted to share all of that. It was a way to reveal that I struggled and still struggle with some of the same things that you do. I figured if one young brother saw himself in my story, then my truth was not in vain. Yes, I did want to share, tell, proclaim, and be transparent about the things I went through on my road to success as a father, an entrepreneur, and a man. I think about the person I wouldn't commit to becoming. I was a figment of my own imagination and time was running out on my charade.

Yes, I was a 30-year-old boy! Physically, I was a man. But mentally, emotionally, and spiritually, I was a boy. I was immature with no goals, plans, or aspirations which showed a lack of mental maturity. I had never been committed to anything or anyone. There lay my lack of emotional maturity. I lacked any spiritual connection. I was raised in the church and my father was a pastor, but that didn't provide me with spiritual maturity. When my daughter, Alonnie, was four, I became a single father, which forced an emotional, mental, and spiritual growth upon me. What was I going to do now? A single father with a little girl who depended on me to raise, teach, protect, and provide for her. How was I going to do those things when I couldn't do them for myself? I think back on how I ended up in that position. Bad decisions and not learning from the results were the main reasons. Inevitably, you're going to make some bad decisions. But what you do after your bad decision is where you develop as a man. Charles R. Swindoll said, "Life is 10% what happens to you and 90% how you react." That means stuff happens, but what are you going to do about it? Will you make the situation worse by making a bad decision? Or, will you formulate a well thought out solution to the situation you've found yourself in? There comes a time when you must stop digging the hole deeper and start building on the ground on which you stand. We have a tendency to make our problems (holes) worse (deeper) with how we react to them. Life has a way of making comfort, uncomfortable. At 30, I had dug such a deep hole for myself; I had no direction, no plan, and no goals. I had to make a turnaround. It wasn't about me anymore. My transformation came in four stages. If you find yourself in a similar situation of not being where you should or need to be, this may help you get on the right track. The turnaround won't happen overnight. It's an infinite process and it is still going on to this day.

Self-Reflection (Reflect: to look back upon)

The first step involved me looking into the rear-view mirror, but I was intently focused on not going back to whatever I saw in that mirror. You have to be very careful when reflecting on your past or you'll repeat it. There also lies an opportunity for regrets and I had plenty. I regretted not committing myself to my education, or anything for that matter. I regretted some of the things I'd done to my mind and my body. I'd wasted most of my adult life playing games and being irresponsible and reckless. At 30, the results of those decisions were staring me right in my face. I couldn't harp on my regrets or allow them to cripple me. Although it was difficult, I had to leave a lot of stuff in the rearview. I had to relieve myself of my failures and disappointments. Some of my closest friends had to be left right where they were, behind me. You see, a true friend wants to see you succeed. But you will find that some friends want you to stay where you are, with them. It validates their lack of success if you're unsuccessful too. I had a friend tell me I spent too much time with my daughter. He was a deadbeat dad whose advice on that topic I knew not to take. So, I knew he wouldn't be going with me! Another friend, after hearing I wanted to pursue my degree, asked me, "What do you want to do that for?" Goodbye friend! I had some bad habits that were hindering my progress. I had to break those chains that were holding me back. There were some good times that came with bad consequences. Some experiences became memories. Some friendships faded. It's really difficult to let go of some things, but in the end, you won't regret the disassociation. Don't spend too much time looking in that mirror or you'll be tempted to go back to where you came from and that place may not be as welcoming as it once was.

Self-Evaluation (Evaluate: to analyze)

You're evaluated throughout your life. Whether it's a test in school or a performance review at work. When you meet someone for the first time, you're evaluating them and being evaluated.

But how often do you honestly evaluate yourself? Self-evaluation for me was thinking about where I stood at that point in my life, where I wanted to be, and how I was going to get there. Yes, I was a single father, but I had a village of family, friends, church, and community that provided the resources I needed. I had a crappy job with no career tract, training, or particular skill set, but at least I had a job and that was a start. I was living paycheck to paycheck, but at least there was a paycheck. I didn't have a degree, certifications, or any formal training, but I was always an intelligent, well-spoken, and well-read brother. That was all the foundation I needed to build upon. We have to be grateful in all situations, good and bad. Although good can and will get better, what if bad got worse? So, through self-evaluation I found myself in a state of gratefulness. Grateful that I was still here with an opportunity to make the best of the life that I was given. A number of my friends were either dead or in jail and the fact that I wasn't, after so many instances where I could've been, was enough to be thankful for. Self-evaluation is difficult because it requires that you be 100 percent honest with yourself about who you are, your struggles, the really good, and the very bad. Self-evaluation is a necessary step in assuring that you have all of the basic components for the success that you desire to achieve.

Self-Improvement (Improve: to make better)

After the evaluation, I began to change some things about myself. I had to or I was destined to repeat the same failings that had me in the position I was in. I began to take my crappy job seriously when one day I went to my supervisor complaining and he told me plainly, "No one is going to give you anything here. If you want it, you have to go get it." That simple statement changed my life and soon after I received a promotion that turned my job into a career. I began to attend church regularly and even joined the choir, and I couldn't sing a lick! That was an amazing experience for me. I was able to fellowship and worship with over 100 men who looked like me and had either been through what I was going through or they were willing to go through it with me. I met my mentors: Rev. Tobias and Rev. Deck. Those were two brothers that I could call on for sound advice, a listening ear, or a word of prayer. They saw things I didn't see in myself and helped me to identify my spiritual gift. Rev. Tobias placed me in charge of the Boys to Men Mentoring Ministry and Rev. Deck chose me as a member of the Men's Council. That was extremely important because a huge part of your success is your willingness to give back. So, at each step on your ladder, be sure to reach back and pull someone up. Having a mentor or mentors is essential to success. A mentor provides so many of the necessary ingredients for success. They provide support, encouragement, wisdom, and experience, amongst so many other things. You can have mentors in every aspect of your journey—spiritual mentors, business mentors, or professional mentors. Most successful people will speak of a mentor or mentors that helped them by providing instructional guidance and support on their path to success. I became an active participant in Alonnie's success. I had to. I was all she had, and she was everything to me. I attended every teacher conference, every boring school play, and every school activity. My village supported me without me even asking. I was determined to be the father that she deserved and the best man I could be.

Self-Preservation (Preserve: to save, maintain)

Now that I had reflected, evaluated, and improved, I had to preserve or maintain who and what I had become and build upon it. I couldn't go back to bad habits that had me in bondage or toxic relationships determined to stifle my success. I had to remain diligent about becoming a better man and a good father. I worked on being consistent. Consistency is key, but it doesn't mean remaining the same. It involves continuing on the path you're on, improving, and growing consistently. The promotion at work led to another and that led to a six-figure salary and 20 years on the job. And to think the day I went to my supervisor complaining, I was considering quitting! I continued attending church regularly and became more involved. I was preserving my success by not falling back into my self-destructive ways. I was growing and maturing. I was no longer a 30 something year old boy. I had started with a foundation, realized through self-evaluation. I built on the small successes that I had, and I was able to forge ahead in building a future for my daughter and myself. The continual pursuit of success and self-preservation eventually led me to start Bow Tie Willie's Bow Ties. I had never sewn in my life, but I needed a bow tie for my wedding and my wife suggested I make it myself. Starting a business wasn't easy and fear of failure and success is real, but you never know what you can do until you do it! Now, three years and hundreds of sales later, I can say that each sale is a success and it's the greatest feeling in the world to see something that I created being worn or in a photograph. And to think, it started with being uncomfortable in my comfort zone and a desire to be successful at something.

As I reflect on my journey, I often think about what I would tell a 16-year-old me. I would say, "Stop doing 'just enough' to get by." Mediocrity is a hindrance to greatness. I would tell myself, "Develop a skill or perfect a talent." You never know how far it might take you. I would definitely tell myself, "Listen to your parents." I didn't realize how smart they were until I grew up. I would say, "Choose your friends carefully." My 16-year-old circle probably wasn't the best; my best friend introduced me to selling drugs when I was in the eleventh grade. The draw of being a fake, part-time hustler, able to buy some fresh tennis shoes and impress some little girls, put me at risk of ruining my future and destroying my life. Fortunately, I was able to make it out of that, but sadly, my best friend wasn't. What would I say to a 21-year-old Will? I'd say, "Finish school. And if school isn't your thing, gain a trade or some sort of training that can propel you to the next level." College isn't for everyone, but knowledge is. I'd tell myself, "Be careful of the bad habits you give power to." Smoking weed, drinking, and partying may seem like the things to do, but trust me, they're not. You're wasting time, destroying your body, and stifling your progress. I would say to myself, "Start thinking about your future, set goals, and make plans." At 30, although my daughter is my greatest blessing, I would say, "Be careful who you love and give yourself to." Sex without love can have drastic results. I'd also tell myself, "Start laying a financial foundation." My father would often say to me: "Will, you're going to look up and you'll be 40 years old with nothing to show for it." I heard him, but I wasn't listening! If I knew then what I know now.

The journey to success is a personal one. You are responsible for your own success and you have your own measures. What one considers a success may not be the same as the next person. Getting a C on a test is success if you typically get an F. Getting a job is a success if you're unemployed. Your first sale as a business owner, graduating from high school, or buying a house are all successes. Success can be the big house or your first apartment. It's the college degree, but also the A on the exam. Material possessions may be marks of success for some, but they don't define it. Success is a feeling, not a possession. Whenever you find yourself stuck or losing focus in your pursuit of success, don't be afraid to take a look in that rearview mirror, reflect on how far you've come, evaluate where you are and where you want to go, improve upon what you have while preserving the successes you've already achieved, then turn around and look to the future with optimism and great expectations for what is ahead of you.

Be blessed and be a blessing!

Mentoring: The Importance of
Being a Servant

Horace L. Moore

In 1997, I started teaching at Rikers Island Detention Center. I was working with young men close to getting their high school diploma or GED. My goal was to positively impact those young men by giving them a second chance. On my first day, as I was escorted to the school area by the Deputy Warden, I heard "Moore" being called out by young men, who I realized were my former middle school students. As a middle school teacher in Brownsville, I was known for my connection with the students and improving their academic levels. Seeing some of my students in Rikers of all places was unsettling for me and it confirmed that work needed to be done for young men before they reached that point.

Unfortunately, my high hopes of affecting change within the prison system were quickly dashed when I realized that there are no constants at Rikers Island. It is a temporary holding location, and progress cannot happen without time and consistency. Just when I would start to connect with a young man, I would learn that he was transferred to another facility. Thankfully, I had enough time with some of the young men for them to know that somebody cared. I felt rewarded when I came into contact with one young man that I taught in middle school and then met again at Rikers years later because he is now working, married, and living a good life. That young man recalled when I was pouring into him and his classmates and telling them, "One in every four boys will end up in jail." Now he does what he can to make a positive difference for others in his community. *The ripple effect of impacting even one person can be wide.*

If someone had told me in high school that I would become an educator and mentor young black men, I would have been certain they were talking about somebody else. However, helping to shape, guide, and develop the minds of tomorrow is my ultimate passion in life. We are the sum of our experiences. The people we cross paths with often impact the decisions we make long after we have encountered them. It is important to recognize these trusted people in your life. You will be able to find them because they will exhibit two key qualities: first, they will consistently interact; second, they will provide guidance with nothing to gain except the joy of servitude. These are mentors, whether formally defined immediately or given that label years later. *Mentors want to see your best self.*

There are many people who poured into me, nurtured my development, and helped mold me into manhood. The adults in my life modeled serving others by sharing love, knowledge, time, and attention with me. As I tried to reflect on the moment or the person that represented my turning point, I realize that my life, like most, has been a series of twists and turns that helped shape my journey thus far. I did not have my father in my life to be a constant example of manhood. What I had from about the age of seven was my mother's good friend, Mr. Po Po. He was a consistent father figure for me. He was a factory worker with limited education, but he always encouraged me to stay in school. He showed sincere care and dedication to help push me into my full potential. Mr. Po Po was my first example of what it looks like to be a man and I will forever be grateful for his consistency. *Mentors want to see you succeed.*

I imagine that Frederick Douglass's words, "It is easier to raise strong children than to repair broken men," must have resonated in the ears of my mentors. In seventh grade, Ms. Allen, my teacher, took on the role of exposing me to new experiences and nurturing my God-given talents. She added an extra hand of parental support and her love planted a seed in me that grew into a desire to make a difference in young people's lives. I will also never forget how much I admired and respected my ninth-grade social studies teacher, Mr. Grant. He was my first black male teacher and he made education fun. If you are looking for guidance or a mentor, look for the person successfully accomplishing their job or goals in a different way and take time to interact with them. For me, that entailed hanging out in Mr. Grant's class and being open to absorbing all the knowledge he had to share. *Look for these types of people as mentors and be receptive to their knowledge and approach with you.*

Although you may have a specific dream for your life, remember that fate may step in. Your mentors and trusted adults may guide you to new opportunities, so be flexible enough to receive your blessings. Most young men from my community strived to play sports professionally or go to the military. Very few were even presented with the opportunity to go to college and I received two college acceptance letters. All I can remember my mother saying was, "That's it, you are going to college." My number one goal was to find my way out and see the world. Overall, I just wanted to try something different. The opportunity to go to college was the result of my willingness to follow the directions of my high school mentors and my mother. Their guidance opened another lane for me. *Mentors introduce opportunities.*

I almost missed one of my most influential male role models during my sophomore year. I remember a black dude approaching me in the college gym saying, "Moore, I need to see you." Now where I am from, if someone wants to "see you," they want to take it outside, and I was not going to allow myself to be ambushed. So, I responded, "No, you can see me right here." Turns out the black dude was my new college advisor, Gregg Nanton, and he just wanted to initiate my first advisory session. Throughout my college years, Mr. Nanton laid the foundation for my transition into manhood by addressing topics like being a man of my word, time management, taking advantage of every educational opportunity, and making solid choices. My advisor became the coach that handed me tools and sharpened my skill set so that I would have a chance at winning in life. *Mentors see the potential in you, often before you see your own potential.*

Do not be dismayed if your first job (or even your first few jobs) does not speak to the core of what you believe you should be doing to make a difference. After my college graduation, I visited Ms. Allen and shared with her that I secured a job working as a financial aid counselor at Suffolk Community College. However, she saw something in me that I had yet to see in myself because her response was, "You are going to teach." Out of love, respect, and reverence for Ms. Allen, I followed her lead as she introduced me to Ernie Logan, a well-respected assistant principal who became a role model and guided me through the process of becoming a teacher. Ms. Allen knew my presence would have a positive impact on the students in Brownsville.

My first teaching position was at the middle school I attended as a child. It was there that I met one of my first students who would refer to me as his mentor. That young man was 13 years old and in my eighth-grade class. I shared a connection with him that grew beyond the classroom. I began to pour into him in the same way that those before me poured into me. Our relationship grew to include his little brother and the two of them looked at me as a father figure. *Remember that establishing positive, trusting relationships is key to effectively serving others.*

Being in those classrooms had as big of an impact on me as it did on the students I was serving. The alarming education gap between my male and female students grew painfully visible to me, as my males were not moving on to high school at the same rate as the females. Those guys were no different from me at their age, but they were not getting what they needed from the school system to excel! That problem ignited a flame in my heart. Charter schools were a new concept to education at that time and my desire to make a difference in young black men's lives motivated me to want to open a school for boys. I spoke to my mentor and spiritual advisor, Reverend Dr. Johnny Ray Youngblood, about my plans. He told me, "Hold on... you are impregnated with an idea, but you have not gone through the labor pains yet."

Sometimes, even your mentor may recommend that you defer your dream because they see your need for additional growth, even though you may not see it. In those times, trust that what is for you will come to pass if you stay focused. My mentor, while telling me to wait for my school, encouraged me to come work at his private school, which turned out to be his way of assessing my work as an educator. Making a switch from the Board of Education to a private school is considered to be career suicide by most. I remember asking myself, "Is this the right thing to do? Is this the right time? Is this a financially sound decision? Will I be able to sustain myself financially?" However, Reverend Youngblood was consistently doing the work of mentoring and empowering men to lead the community, and he sat with me to help me develop my plan to mentor and develop future generations of young men. *Your passion and sacrifice to make a difference along with trust in your advisor or mentor can pave the way to your alternative route to success.*

Often times, transitional plans are in God's plan. My mentorship program, Chionesu Bakari (CB), was a transitional plan that started as a summer program. It felt like a consolation prize for me not starting the all-boys charter school in 2004. I do not take no as a final answer, even when the road may take a detour. As a result of remaining focused on my passion with keen determination to pour into young black men, CB's summer program is now a year-round uniformed program with a 100 percent high school graduation rate and a 96 percent college acceptance rate. I have shaped a program built on the mission of reclaiming, re-naming, renewing, and reconditioning the minds of young men by mentoring, exposure, and a curriculum that includes expertise inside and outside of CB.

Reverend Youngblood played a major role in bringing CB to fruition, as he sat with me to help me figure out the best people to get to work with me that first summer. He helped me lay the groundwork for determining what would make the program most impactful for the young men we were going to serve. That process took energy and spiritual work to discern what was needed versus what was not needed. He taught me that I needed to select like-minded people who would take my vision on as their own. I'm grateful for the current staff Victor Young, Vaughn Curmon, Keir Nelson, Susan Del Moor, and other men and women that have been on staff with me. Each of them has not only supported the vision but have embodied and dedicated themselves to the development of the program.

Throughout that first summer and into the first year, we learned a few things, set the mission statement, honed in on mentoring the whole young man, including their family, and shaped what would become the core curriculum areas: character and skills development and decision-making. The program gave the young men a voice, resources, and the attention that they so desperately needed. In addition, we discovered in order to effectively serve the young men, CB needed to develop families and relationships. We had to recognize as mentors the source of our mentee's challenges and open the success of the program to the engagement of a young men's family. This is not an easy calling, however, to serve as leaders, we have to follow where the need arises. Especially if we are making change in a larger way, in CB's case, building positive family dynamics and community. We were on the forefront, but we were doing God's work. Soon, we realized that CB could not just be a summer program and the year-round mentorship program was born! *Mentors serve to help develop S.M.A.R.T. (Specific, Measurable, Achievable, Relevant, Timely) plans of action.*

Looking back and reflecting on starting out with nothing and bearing witness to where CB is today confirms that trusting the process is key. Throughout the years, CB has been operating out of St. Paul Community Baptist Church under the spiritual leadership of Rev. David K. Brawley. I am truly grateful for the continuous spiritual and financial covering from Pastor Brawley and the members of St. Paul Community Baptist Church. In many ways, St. Paul has been a Godsend for the growth of CB, the young men, parents, and staff alike.

My journey from the challenges of my youth in Brownsville, Brooklyn, to allowing myself, sometimes stubbornly, to be guided by mentors led me to my success now. From that journey, I created a blueprint for building a successful life of servitude, mentoring, and making a difference in the lives of others. This blueprint may sound cliché, but here it is: Never give up! Find your group of people that will give you sound advice. Make sure they are capable of holding you accountable and telling you when you are wrong. Have a determination to serve even during times when you may not be getting paid. Have a love for what you do and, at minimum, an equal dose of love for the people that you serve. Surround yourself with people who can see your vision and take it on as their own. And, lastly trust your process.

Be All You Can Be . . . and Then Some

Frank N. Sanders

In the beginning, everything seemed so simple. Growing up as a kid in the late 1970's in Albany, New York, was all about watching Saturday morning cartoons, Kung Fu Theater, and then going outside to emulate on one of my homeboys what we just watched Bruce Lee do. Television and comic books were my escape from the everyday grind of house chores, school, and the relentless onslaught of playing the dozens with my friends. We were the products of *School House Rock*, *ABC Afterschool Specials*, and yes, who can forget the TV show *Good Times*! My reality came from my family. I was an only child up until the age of nine. My mother adopted my three cousins, whom I have always considered my brothers and sister. It wasn't uncommon back then for a family to take in other family members in time of need. My mom didn't believe that a State Foster Care Agency could take care of family better than family, especially for black children. We were educated in a private school, which was an experience in itself. The teachers were predominantly white, but the student population was predominantly black. Those teachers pushed us harder than any others. A few teachers revealed to us that they marched with Dr. Martin Luther King Jr. during The Civil Rights Movement. Maybe they knew our struggles as black people and wanted better for us.

I had a stepfather who was in the picture mostly as a disciplinarian, but he gave me and my siblings the drive to stay focused on education and making money "the right way." His "right way" was stay out of the afterhours clubs, don't drink alcohol, don't do or sell drugs, and most importantly… "Stay away from them girls!" I later found out after he passed away that he made most of his income by doing those same things he forbid us to do, but that is for another story. So, I earned money the old-fashioned way. My brothers and I would work around the neighborhood by raking leaves in the fall and shoveling snow in the winter. Then in the summer, we would apply for jobs with the city's summer youth programs. I liked having money in my pocket. I was very frugal with money and didn't spend it all at once. Let my brothers tell the story, I still got my lunch money from the third grade! We had an uncle who lived with us also and he was like our big brother. He was a college student and the first black man in my family that influenced me to pursue higher education after high school. As the years passed, we lived modestly, but the challenges of life began to change my mindset. My mother developed health problems which limited her ability to work full time. Around the same time, my grandmother became ill and she eventually moved in with us.

By this time, my brothers and I were in our teens and we were ready to hit the streets. In the early to mid-1980s, Albany's summers were full of block parties, community festivals, skating rinks, and cookouts. Somebody was always having a cookout! As a young black male, I wanted to experience it all. My mom, still trying to be the disciplinarian, would tag team with my grandmother and try to whoop us for staying out late. Now, it wouldn't have been bad if my grandmother wasn't half blind and hitting a chair with a belt thinking it was us! (Y'all going to hell if you laughed.) Out of respect, we would honor my mother's punishment of being grounded for a weekend, but would somehow convince her to let us go out if we promised we would be home before the streetlights came on. My mother established a reverence for God in our lives at an early age by requiring us to go to church on Sundays. Church was the first time I heard messages about understanding your purpose in life and preordained destiny, which I would later fall back on.

By the mid to late 80's, hip hop culture became my influence because it touched on the political and social issues that impacted urban communities and focused on the realities that many young black males were experiencing. Ghetto life, drugs, poverty, racism, and partying were often the topics of discussion resonating from boom boxes throughout my hood in rhythmic harmony and I was hooked! Hip hop became my institution of higher learning. My professors were: Run-D.M.C., KRS-One, Doug E. Fresh, Slick Rick, Public Enemy, LL Cool J, and Big Daddy Kane, just to name a few. And during that new renaissance of music and cultural awareness came an era of crack cocaine. The group of friends I grew up with started changing. By that time, every young black male I grew up with was a part of a single parent household, with women being the sole breadwinners. My role models were my peers who either converted into Five Percenters, drug dealers, or plain old hustlers. I never became any of those, maybe because I knew it would have killed my mother if she found out. I couldn't bear the hurt it would've caused, especially with her being ill. So, I would hang out with my friends finding pick-up basketball games or we would just spark up an "el" and pass around a 40 oz. of malt liquor. When it was time for my homies to get into some criminal activities, someone would laugh and say to me, "Yo... ain't it time for you to go home?" The older teens would tell me straight up, "This ain't for you." Deep down I felt they had my best interest in mind and knew my home situation. I never tried to fit in where I didn't belong. I enjoyed "that life" but I wasn't "about that life."

The Crossroads

Life doesn't always go the way we plan it. There are times when life's simplicities become complicated and the fabric of a person's character is tested. In Albany, New York, in the mid to late 80's, money wasn't a problem. At least for the people I knew. Legally or illegally, either way, people was getting it. The summer before I entered my senior year of high school, my mother's health turned for the worse and she wanted us closer to family in Reading, Pennsylvania, because she knew she didn't have that much time left. My two brothers left first, and my sister and I stayed with my mother until the final move at the end of the summer. The life that I knew forever changed. Reading, Pennsylvania, was a culture shock to me. It had its ups and downs. All my family that I visited over the years during the summers and holidays were now at my leisure. While everyone was enjoying their final year in high school, I was assimilating to a new school environment as well as watching my mother's health deteriorate.

I would call back to Albany, New York, to see who was doing what. Then all of a sudden, the stories started changing. People I grew up with were being swallowed up by the crack epidemic. Homeboys I grew up with were going to jail for selling crack, being killed, or becoming crack addicts. I definitely wasn't about that life. Over the next few years I had to grow up fast. My mom (my solid foundation) passed away in spring of 1987, the year after I graduated from high school. I could still hear her voice telling me, "Make something of yourself" and "Be all you can be." That latter phrase was like an epiphany when I heard it again on a television commercial promoting enlistment into the United States Army. By that time, I was in a relationship with a young lady and had a son. I got a decent job working at an insurance company and settled for the norm. But crack had migrated and spread like a plague throughout the northeast. Even the slow- paced city of Reading was no match for the carnage it left upon the residents.

Again, I had friends and family members who were drug dealers and the money looked good, but it had its consequences. Seeing friends and close family members being taken by drugs was too much. Innocent bystanders were being gunned down erratically like military combatants. I had to get out! So out of the blue, I went and spoke to an Army recruiter to "be all I could be." I wanted to get as far away as possible from all the hurt and pain that was constantly being rendered on me daily. I wanted something better for me and my family. So I enlisted in the Army, took my family, and started my new life as an enlisted Soldier.

Depending on your MOS (Military Occupation Specialty), a job in the Army is almost equivalent to a civilian job of the same statute. However, the rigorous technical and tactical training in preparation for combat is like none other. Leaving Reading was the best thing that could happen to me, so I thought. Now I had a structural foundation, purpose, direction, and motivation to "be all I could be." But something was still missing. As a young man I appreciated the virtue of discipline because I was taught that it could lead to greater self-improvement. That was the Army's philosophy; they would tear you down to build you up... by any means necessary. Back then, the Army didn't embrace the concept of family like it does today. You would hear Senior Enlisted NCOs sarcastically say, "If the Army wanted you to have a wife, it would have issued you one!" Young men were getting married, but they didn't anticipate the hardships of Army life plus juggling the responsibilities of being a provider, father, and husband. Many young Soldiers fell victim to the stereotypical persona of what a man is supposed to be—a player or a pimp! I struggled with being a husband and a provider for my family, and I was still mourning the loss of my mother.

For many young Soldiers, just like marriage, divorce is a part of Army life. Soldiers are counseled by their supervisors or peers to "Suck it up and drive on." I was one of those soldiers. As the years passed, I didn't try to understand the behavior that led to my divorce. I just took the L and kept it moving. I loved my first-born son, but I wasn't going to go through the baby momma drama. That was unproductive for my military career and my future relationship with my son. I took care of him financially, but I couldn't be there for him physically. That always bothered me. I still wanted my family, but I knew that the strain of the Army would take its toll again. I got older and continued up the enlisted ranks. I'd adapted to the required roles and responsibilities placed upon me by my superiors. I felt confident in my abilities as a Soldier and I appreciated the opportunity to serve my country. Relationship wise, I continued to date and got into a serious relationship and had another son. This time I was going to get it right! Everything was perfect, so I thought. Part of being in a relationship is that both parties must have the same vision and be spiritually compatible. Again… I took an L and kept it moving, but this time my son came with me.

Moving Ahead

I was now a single parent! My contract was up for the Army and I didn't reenlist because I knew the demands of my position would take me away from my son. I still loved the Army, but I put him first. With my new sense of purpose, I finally embraced the slogan: "Be All That You Can Be." I focused my entire existence on being a good father and provider for my sons. I thought back on the message Understanding Your Purpose in Life and began my journey to become a role model for my sons and impact the lives of other young males. I focused on God and His purpose for my life and everything started prospering. With wisdom, knowledge, and understanding came prosperity. I became a lifelong learner and received my first college degree. I read books that inspired me to create wealth. Then, I purchased my first income property, which was the first of many goals I set for myself in hopes that my sons would one day mimic my behavior. The Army taught me to lead by example, so I set my actions to do so. It wasn't about me anymore; it was about my sons and providing an inheritance for their future. Like my mother instilled in me, I found a good church that gave me a firm foundation for developing a personal relationship with God and taught me how to walk in the spirit of excellence. In the Bible, Matthew 6:33 (NIV) reads, "But seek first his kingdom and his righteousness, and all these things will be given to you as well." God knew the desires of my heart and as time passed, I remarried and was blessed again with four additional sons.

With this new revelation, I felt confident and understood my life's purpose. I was motivated to be the best provider for my family and I found opportunities to help others as well. I was fortunate to work as a supervisor for juvenile detention centers in Anchorage, Alaska; Paterson, New Jersey; and St. Louis, Missouri. I was told later that my recently discovered purpose propelled other men to break generational reviles and be the Dads they never had to their children. That's what it's all about, making a positive impact that will influence people. After 9/11, I was motivated to return to Active Duty. So with the support of my wife (who is actively serving in the Army), I reenlisted into the Army. My faith, strength, and courage were tested when I deployed to Iraq in 2009 for 10 months. It was a very humbling experience, but I knew God's purpose for me so being in a war zone was just another testimony for me to share. For the next ten years, I continued serving in the Army while being stationed throughout the United States and overseas. During my time in the Army, I persistently embraced the motto: "Be All That You Can Be." So, I served my country, pursued more education, raised my sons, purchased several real estate properties, and built positive relationships with people all around the world.

I finally retired from the Army in 2018 and now I'm pursuing my dream of starting my own real estate management company. Understanding your purpose means waking up excited about the opportunities that are waiting for you each day. I determined in my mind to positively impact at least one person I come in contact with daily. Share your stories and life experiences, and network with like-minded people. Planting one small seed of knowledge into someone could change their entire future and impact generations to come.

Finally, "Believe in your heart that you're meant to live a life full of passion, purpose, magic and miracles."—Roy T. Bennett

This will set you apart from everyone else. Peace!

How to Be a Thief Amongst Wolves

Mendel Murray

There is a cliché that life has its ups and downs. Clichéd, but true. As we go through life, we face a number of unfortunate experiences: loss, rejection, failure, and disappointment to name a few. Everyone has experienced those feelings. It's what unites us. The underlying question is: How do we deal with such adversity? My answer is to take each moment, internalize it, and no matter how many times you get knocked down, get back up. I know from personal experience. Growing up, I always wondered how I could steal success in a world that didn't want me to have it in the first place. It was from that thought that I set out on my journey to make a small difference in a big world.

It was the fall semester of my first year in middle school. I was in Mr. Perez's art class. I was not popular in any sense of the word, but I wanted to be. I was doing a drawing of Michael Jackson and a girl I liked leaned over to me and said, "Mendel, it would be really funny if you took those dirty gym pants and put them on that boy's head over there." That boy was the biggest kid in the class, but I wanted so much to fit in and impress her that I obliged and said, "Okay, cool, yeah that would be pretty funny." I can't tell you the joy that came over me when she suggested that I pull that prank, let alone that she even spoke to me. Scared but determined, I did it. Everyone, of course, laughed. Although I felt proud and self-satisfied, I must admit that there was something within the pit of my stomach that told me I had used poor judgment. Time to move on, right? Wrong. Moments later, the target of the prank, the biggest guy in the class, got even by wiping my face with the dirty shorts and tying them around my head. Disgusted and embarrassed, I said to him, "Watch when we get to the next class. I'm gonna beat you up so badly." Remember this kid was twice my size, so I was really taking a risk. What made matters worse was the "cool kids" whose approval I wanted and for whom I was performing had already been kicked out of class. In a matter of fifteen minutes, I had lost my audience and my dignity. I then said in my head, "Mendel, who are you really trying to impress?" From that day forward, I became the quiet kid, a shell of my former self.

In high school, I had the reputation of being the quiet kid. I tacitly sought the approval of my peers by wearing name brand clothing that I couldn't afford and allowing malingerers to copy my homework. At times, I neglected my own academics to help them with theirs. When I finally got to twelfth grade, I suffered with the reality that my intermittent neglect had seriously impacted my own transcript and college acceptances. This time rejection didn't come at the hands of my peers, but at those of colleges and universities. While all of my friends were being accepted into big time colleges and the Armed Forces, I was on a fast track to nowhere because my priorities were screwed up. Two weeks before graduation, I was finally accepted to the University of Bridgeport (UB). I graduated from high school with a 2.5 grade point average and was headed to Bridgeport, Connecticut, to try and make something of my life. I wanted to prove that UB did not make an unwise decision by accepting me, that I had learned my lesson, and that I was no longer at the mercy of wanting anyone's approval but my own.

When I first stepped foot on the campus of the University of Bridgeport, I never imagined it would have as big of an impact as it did. It was there that I realized the most valuable lesson: the idea of finding myself was nonsense. It was much more important for me to know who I was not than for me to know who I was. I was not a follower; I was not a party goer; I was not a malingerer. I was also not immune to the utter despair that comes from a broken romance.

I had a girlfriend one minute, and then I didn't. It was heartbreaking—more than I realized. I was depressed. Me, the guy with all the ambition and drive, the one who did not need anyone else's approval, the one with everything to live for—a loving family, a sense of my future—for a moment, stared at a kitchen knife and wondered if he had anything to live for. The next day, I looked for the same knife just to convince myself that I wasn't dreaming, but I couldn't find it. The whole episode left me frightened and uncertain. I would look at myself in the mirror, thinking and believing that I was ugly. I went days without eating. I had painful chest palpitations because of the anxiety I felt every time the phone rang. I lost a lot of weight and had major self-esteem issues, all because I didn't know how to deal with the breakup of a relationship. It was a revelation. 2015 was the worst year of my life. Suicidal thoughts, depression, and anxiety plagued my life. I was in hell for an entire year.

But then things started looking up. Well, mostly. I got involved with the UB basketball team as
the manager, began networking with people in
the business school, and made some new friends.
Then, I got a scholarship from the UB alumni committee. Prior to getting that phone call, I had been
rejected from three internship programs with the
Brooklyn Nets, the NBA, and another scholarship
program from UB. On September 14, 2016, however, I was awarded a $10,000 scholarship from the
alumni board. I was asked to make a few remarks.
Sitting in the audience was a man who changed
the course of my life and my career. That man was
Bill Manning, the president of the Toronto FC and
an alumnus of UB. Impressed by my speech, Mr.
Manning said he wanted to get to know me better.
We kept in contact, and he invited me to Toronto.
He paid for my flight to meet with the president of
the Toronto Raptors, Masai Ujiri, and members of
the Toronto FC staff. Before I left, the best advice
I received came from Aditya Sharma who told me,
"Whatever you do, make sure you make the trip
back as soon as possible. No matter what it is for,
you must keep these relationships alive." Taking
his advice, one month later, I set out to take a va-
cation in Toronto. I reached out to everyone I had
met and to the assistant to the general manager

who said to me, "I will not be in Toronto, but I will be in New York for one of our road games. You are welcome to join me." Of course, I went, and I sat in a luxury suite at Yankee Stadium. Imagine me. The young man that almost killed himself a year prior was sitting in a luxury suite in Yankee Stadium. How crazy is that. The next morning, I caught a flight to Toronto, and I met with people at Toronto FC and took in the sights and sounds of Toronto with my sister while catching a game with my mentor Bill.

Throughout life two of the biggest questions we all have to answer are: What am I good at? and What makes me unique? While I am still figuring those things out, I have come to some conclusions. I am good at networking and branding. I have taken all of the advice from my connections and leveraged it to get in contact with people all around the NBA. From different teams to the NBA headquarters, I touched on everyone I could including commissioner Adam Silver and deputy commissioner Mark Tatum. Speaking with those people and knowing graduation was right around the corner, I jumped at the chance to attend a career fair at the Barclays Center in Brooklyn. I paid $143.00 to enter, and it put me in front of the right people to get the job I have today with the Brooklyn Nets.

The franchise that had rejected me three times was now offering me a position.

It is important to realize that things happen for a reason but not necessarily when you want them to. This journey has allowed me to meet so many people. From local business owners to CEOs of major corporations, I have made many important contacts in the fields of business, politics, sports, and entertainment.

One of my favorite quotes comes from John Wayne. It says, "Courage is being scared to death and saddling up anyways." This short story of my journey has put me in a position to help other young people with similar stories. I know they are out there. Suicidal thoughts scared me, depression scared me, and anxiety scared me. But here I am. And I am better for having had those experiences.

I'm only 22 and I want to be an advocate for young people. I understand the worries they face. I understand the journey ahead and the challenges that might discourage them. The scary thing about troubled kids is that they look like normal young people. When I went through my depression, my grades were great so you couldn't tell. I didn't have any friends on campus, so who would have noticed? I could have been dust in the wind without a soul to remember my name.

So why am I still here? My spiritual answer is that God is not finished with me yet. As you look at my life now, I have touched the lives of youth through mentorship and have brought groups of people together to share my story. The point is, if you are here, God has a plan for you. I'm not here to preach to you, but think about it... I never did find that knife again.

My message to young people is:

1. As you go through life many people will tell you that you cannot do things, but oftentimes people that tell you that are those who have failed in their own goals. Whatever you think is attainable probably is, but you cannot be discouraged by failure when you haven't even begun to climb the mountain.

2. No mountain is without its crags. There are many obstacles and roadblocks that will try to interrupt your journey to success. It is up to you to decide what will stop you and what will make you keep going.

3. Success is often the warmest place to hide. Do not pay attention to other people and think you are failing because you are not where they are. Get out of the matrix

that is social media! Everyone's journey is different, and everyone's path is different. (You'll notice that you see only people's successes because people never post their failures.) So, never measure your success by anyone else's. Be proud of your own successes—no matter how big or how small they are.

4. Pablo Picasso once said, "When I was a child my mother said to me, 'If you become a soldier, you'll be a general. If you become a monk, you'll be the pope.' Instead I became a painter and wound up as Picasso." Today, whenever one hears the name Picasso, they think of an iconic painter. What are you going to do that your name will change the game? Whatever you love to do, strive to be the best.

It's Not Too Late

Randall E. Toby

I was very angry with my father while growing up. I didn't remember him calling me to see how I was doing, coming by to visit, or offering to spend the day with me. What made matters worse was having to read articles about him in *JET magazine* (An African American entertainment publication) or being interviewed occasionally in *The New York Times*, *Daily News*, or *New York Post*.

I was raised by a single mother. Prior to graduating from high school, she and my grandmother informed me that neither of them could afford to buy a suit for me for the occasion. I was really disappointed, so my grandmother suggested, "Why don't you go ask your father?" Who, me? *She must be kidding*, I thought to myself. I barely knew the man. Well, one week later I found myself heading to his job located at 26 Federal Plaza in lower Manhattan. When I arrived at his office, I informed his secretary at the front desk who I was.

The woman seemed quite surprised. (My younger brothers, Michael and Kenny, later told me that many of his colleagues and friends didn't know that he had an older son.) As I entered his large, well-decorated office, I couldn't help but notice the many prominently displayed awards and thank you letters he had received from a variety of politicians and business leaders from around the world. As I approached his oversized desk, he shook my hand.

The first words he uttered were, "Why is it that the only time I hear from you is when you want something?" He seemed to be annoyed by my mere presence. I was devastated. He opened his wallet and handed me a fifty-dollar bill. I was so hurt that I can't remember what happened next; I felt as though I was in a daze. It was as if he had physically punched me in my chest.

Somehow, I made my way onto the elevator and headed outside of his building where I immediately broke down and cried uncontrollably. The words he uttered ripped me apart. I had never asked him for anything in my entire life. What was he referring to? I was both embarrassed and humiliated. From that very moment on, I felt a deep hatred for my father. He lit a competitive fire, one that still burns inside of me today.

I told myself that I would never speak to him again. I was determined to be successful on my own, maybe even become wealthy. *I'll show him*, I thought to myself. Research has shown that a father being absent during a child's adolescence can have an impact on the child's life that includes recognizing limits, learning the roles of social interactions, and an increased tendency to engage in delinquency. The Fatherhood Project, a non-profit program, found in their 2018 research that children who have a closer relationship with their father have a higher chance of entering college or finding stable employment after high school. They are also 75 percent less likely to have a teen birth, 80 percent less likely to spend time in jail, and half as likely to experience multiple depression symptoms. Many single mothers do a great job raising their children; however, there are subtle differences. A woman typically is more nurturing, gentle, comforting, protective, and gives great emotional support to her children.

More than 20 years had passed since the incident at my father's office, when one day I received an invitation to attend his retirement party being held at the Rainbow Room, located at 30 Rockefeller Plaza in New York. I couldn't help but think, "Why me? Why now?" I spoke to my wife who encouraged me to attend, but I had mixed feelings. I told her it was too late, and I wanted nothing to do with the man. However, as I later wrote in my book, *Toby's Tips: Lessons I've Learned Before it Was Too Late*, "A good woman makes a good man great." So, I followed her advice. During the event, one of my father's friends, Charles Rangel, who was a US Representative in New York and a guest speaker, introduced my father to the audience. He thanked his colleagues, government officials, friends, and business associates. Then, he said my name. Finally! After all those years, he acknowledged my existence. Suddenly, a feeling of inner peace overcame me. I can't explain it, but I forgave him at that very moment.

Not long after attending my father's retirement celebration, he made a huge effort to become a part of my life. He would often say to me, "Son, I am very proud of you." I later learned from him that he grew up very poor. At age 12, he ran away from home in Savannah, Georgia, to escape a cruel stepmother. He lived with an uncle in Harlem, New York. At age 16, in 1951, he dropped out of high school, lied about his age, and joined the Air Force during the heat of the Korean War. He served for four years. During that time, he attended night school in London, England, earned a General

Education Diploma (GED), and took advantage of the G.I. Bill to attend college.

My father earned a bachelor's degree in Spanish from West Virginia State University and held advanced certificates in Spanish from the Universities of Leon and Toledo in Spain. He attained a master's degree in health administration from Harvard University's John F. Kennedy School of Government and a master's degree in social work from Adelphia University.

The federal government adopted a policy of affirmative action to open doors for African Americans who had been barred from professional positions in government and the private sector. In 1968, my father was selected by a competitive process to become a manager in the U.S. Department of Health & Human Services.

By 1992, my father had reached the pinnacle of success in the federal government when President George H. Bush appointed him as the acting administrator of the Federal Health Care Financing Administration in Washington (now the Centers for Medicare and Medicaid Services). In April of 2018, my father passed, just short of his eighty-second birthday.

What I learned from our relationship was that hardships are meant to challenge you not to stop you and it's never too late to repair a relationship, start a business, purchase a home, find a new job, or even get married. Why do people stop dreaming or dream less as they grow older? Why do they lose hope or let the fire inside of them burn out? You don't have to. For example, there was a couple who created dining surveys. Their restaurant guides became so popular that the husband, Tim, quit his job as a corporate attorney to manage the business at the age of 51. His wife, Nina, eventually left her job as well and their company, Zagat, was purchased by Google for $151 million in 2011.

At what age do you feel you should be successful? At what point in your life should you realize that your dream will not come true or you should just stop dreaming all together? NEVER.

There is no set timeline for when success will strike. For most of us, our 20's are a blur of job-hopping and career mistakes. And while it certainly may not feel like it at the time, those years can prove to be crucial to building a successful future.

Let's look at the career of actress Kerry Washington who worked at a restaurant, taught yoga, and was a New York City substitute teacher before she landed her breakout role at 35 years old as Olivia Pope on the hit TV series Scandal. It's even possible to succeed at something you've never done before. Donald Fisher was 40 years old when he and his wife decided to open a store without any prior experience in retail. The first store was opened in San Francisco, California, and became a tremendous success. The GAP Inc. is a leading global apparel retail company. They offer apparel, accessories, and personal care products under the Gap, Banana Republic, Old Navy, Athleta, and Intermix brands.

If you want to become a dream chaser regardless of your age, then you can't be afraid of rejection. The most successful goal setters understand that failure is a lesson in disguise; you must be willing to evolve and adjust your game plan, not quit. People who give up on their goals stay entirely too attached to what their vision was at the onset. They are unwilling to compromise with the new information their journey has provided. They would rather chalk it all up as a failed venture than take what they've learned along the way, apply it, and allow their idea to change shape. Most of the time, people give up on their goals simply because they lack discipline. They can't get themselves to see something through to the end, regardless of how small the project. They haven't yet cultivated the habits required to work not just on the days they feel inspired, but on the days they feel uninspired as well.

Should being over 40 deter you from wanting more? No! Back in 2010, according to Forbes, two of the fastest growing tech startups were First Solar, founded by a 68-year-old, followed by Riverbed Technology, co-founded by entrepreneurs who were 51 and 33 at the time. Research has shown that entrepreneurs who started their business when they were older had a significant chance of being successful.

Let's look at relationships. US statistics on gender, age, and marital status reveal that for increasing years after forty, the percentage of single women rises as compared to single men. However, it is possible to find someone special to share your life with as you get older. Here are some tips on how to start dating after 40:

Before starting, know your worth – God has a plan, but you must be cautious when dating because there are a lot of angry, broken, and wounded people in the world. Take your time getting to know your date and go slow.

Volunteer at places that interest you – Check out community activities and local food banks, or get involved with your local church, synagogue, or mosque. You will often find like-minded people who have interests similar to yours.

Consider relocating – If you have the ability to be flexible, consider relocating. There are some smaller-sized towns that have active social groups. If you want an active social life, maybe it's important to move to places where there are lots of people like you.

Reconnect with people you once knew – Life is constantly changing. Often times, someone you grew up with or knew from college may have gone through a divorce or become a widow or widower.

Ask someone out – Finally, if you meet someone interesting, it's okay to ask them out for a cup of coffee. In fact, it's almost better to ask them outright than to overdo it on the flirting and appear to be desperate.

We all have dreams and thoughts on things we want to do or have in life. Most of us reflect on them often, imagining and wishing they could become reality. So many people sit in their cubicle at work or on their couch in their pajamas daydreaming and then formulating reasons why it's too late to do anything about them.

Here are some of the excuses people make:

- My friends and family will think I'm crazy.
- I have to sacrifice too much to make it happen.

- I'm too old.

- I'm too busy.

- I don't have enough money.

- I'm not smart enough.

- I'm not ready.

It's really sad and disappointing when you allow people to stop you from pursuing what you want. What's even worse is when you become your own dream killer. Do you know the story of the woman that once viewed herself as a failure? Her marriage had ended, and she was unemployed raising an infant daughter. But she recounts her failure as a sort of release, allowing her to focus on her passion of writing.

After completing the first book manuscript while on government aid (public assistance), manually typed copies were submitted to 12 publishers. It was rejected by them all.

She didn't give up. The collection of *Harry Potter* movies has earned more than $7 billion in combined global box office sales, not including the book. Her name is J. K. Rolling.

There are so many people who had someone try to influence them and dissuade them from pursuing their aspirations, but they were successful anyway because they kept the dream alive, they continued chasing their goals.

Are you afraid to look for a new job? You might be older, but with age comes wisdom. As a career coach, I've noticed that some of the clients over 40 years old that hire me allowed fear to hold them back. Do you have the qualifications? Can you bring value to the position? If you're a subject matter expert or have specific skills, play that up in your resume, cover letter, or communications with a recruiter. It's easy to focus on why you can't get the job, but the trick is to not let that keep you from even trying. You still may have time to make a lateral move to gain new skills or to learn an industry you may not have been in yet.

Just sending your resume to career websites will do nothing for you. The tip here is to use your network of colleagues, former business associates, and friends to find companies who are hiring and will have a genuine interest in what we can do for their organizations.

Much to the disbelief of some, age doesn't have to stifle your tech knowledge. Especially not in today's society. Most of us already use work related apps like Zoom, Dropbox, and others. The point is, take a class or get a certification so that there is no excuse for companies or managers not to give you an opportunity.

Try not to be discouraged by the difficulties involved in a midlife career change. If you want to make a transition, try to find a way to do it that fits with your current life situation. It may take a bit longer than it would have if you were ten years younger, but if you do it right, it will likely be worthwhile.

Is there something in the back of your mind that keeps hinting that you are meant for more? Do you ever think that life has something greater in store for you? What are you capable of? Are you wondering if you're accomplishing everything God has set out for you to do?

Don't doubt that living the life you dream of is within your control. Start working towards your dream today because it's never too late.

Who Said You Can't Do That?

DJ Tony Tone

Behind the Ropes: Born to Do This

Growing up in the South Bronx, the home of hip hop, I didn't know GOD was setting me up. You see, I come from a very big family and I mean big. Thank you to the Simmons, Daniels, and Hayward families. Family, love, and music were parts of my childhood and the start of my music career.

Before I go any further, let me give a shout out to JP. He was one of the neighborhood DJs who gave me my fix, or should I say my first shot. JP was one of the DJs who would set up his equipment and plug into the streetlights for power to play music in the park. That is where my passion and love for music came from. After playing basketball with friends and seeing JP set up, my energy went to another level. Time after time, I was fascinated with the sounds and crowds that would come out to the park just to hear JP and MC's do what they loved.

One day, JP saw me standing next to the ropes and he let me come on the other side behind the ropes. OH OH OH!!! What a feeling. Now I felt like I belonged. Wait, it gets better.

So, one time while at the park jam, JP asked me to get on the set. I played about 15 minutes, but it felt like an hour or two. I was hooked. That was what I wanted to do for the rest of my life, but I didn't know GOD was showing me my gift. Looking back, it all started by those ropes.

Discipline and Patience: You Must Work While You Wait

Fast forward. Like I said, I have a big family so during family reunions, birthday parties, or holiday celebrations, I was able to play music and work on my skills. It never seemed like a burden to me, in fact it's what makes me happy and fulfilled.

Throughout my younger days either I was playing music or basketball, or spending time with the ladies. Sometimes the ladies had more of my attention than the music, that's a whole other story, but eventually I got back on track. You see, when GOD has gifted you and created you for a purpose (Jeremiah 1:5), nothing you try or put before HIM will satisfy you. Trust me, I have tried different jobs, relationships, and even drugs, but nothing gave me peace. We were created to have a relationship with the Almighty, and anything that disturbs that will cause hurt, pain, and confusion. I'm not trying to preach, I'm just sharing from my personal experience that when I put number one where number one belongs, everything else lines up.

Success never comes overnight. It is based on time, preparation, and opportunity. The more time you have to prepare, the better the opportunities. Preparation is the key because it's the only part of those three that you are responsible for. No one can prepare for you. Too many people want the fast track to success. Truth is there is no such thing. Even if you take a shortcut to something, you're still spending time trying to figure out how to get around doing it. Wouldn't it just be better to invest that time into understanding how to do it the right way? There is a gift inside of each and every person. GOD made us that way. Seek Jesus Christ to know what your gift is and be the best version of you!

Start Where You Can: Where You Are Now is Not the End

They say, "Never despise small beginnings" and that is so true. A seed planted in the ground can take years to grow into a large tree bearing fruit, so it's not wise to be upset with the seed while it's growing underground where no one can see what's happening. It's the same with the process of being successful. Sometimes you have to begin in a place that does not see the value of what's inside of you. That's ok. If you keep going and remain dedicated, over time people will see what you knew all along. Your starting place is often helping you to develop your gift.

That was the case for me. I started out on the promotions team with WLIB and WBLS while we were over at Park Avenue and 34th. Street. That was my start in radio. Shout out to DJ Mitch "The People Plezzer" for giving me a chance. You see, when you are focused and determined, GOD will put the right people in your life to help you on your journey. While I was in promotions, I looked for any and every opportunity to showcase my gift. I remember my first Circle of Sisters event with WBLS. I was scheduled to play but something happened the night before with the equipment. Mitch called me the day I was supposed to play and said I would have to bring my own DJ set up. That was a big problem because I was just coming out of church service at Christian Cultural Center (C.C.C.) in Brooklyn and at the time I was living in the Bronx. I had to figure out how I was going to get to the Bronx from Brooklyn and then to the Jacob Javits Center in Manhattan in enough time. But, like I have been saying, when you put GOD first, everything else lines up. Needless to say, the Lord made a way for me to get there on time.

There I was in front of thousands of people doing what I loved. People were watching, but they didn't know who I was. You see, when you arc called to do something, you are not concerned with who is watching or who knows you, you just want the opportunity to do what you love.

That was the beginning of many successful runs with WBLS and WLIB. I will forever be grateful to them for giving me my start in radio. The relationships I have built will last a lifetime. The world is smaller than people think, so the relationships you keep on the good side can come back to be a blessing later on in life. A seed has many other seeds inside of it, so where you plant it does matter.

Obstacles Are for You to Overcome

Life is full of challenges. Some are from without, many are within.

If you are ever going to do something of significance, trust and believe it will be met with obstacles. That is a surefire way to test whether you are called to do something, to test your motives, or to see if it was just a good idea. Some people give up after the first obstacle that comes their way, others press through because there is no turning back. Obstacles are not meant to stop you, they are there to help you grow and clearly examine your why.

You see, a lot of people never examine why they are doing something. One thing I have learned over the years is that every time something became a challenge for me, I had to refocus and ask myself, "Why are you doing this?" When you're honest with yourself after asking that question, you will be in a position to get through or grow through whatever challenges are trying to stop you. That is what I had to do when a setback happened when proposing *Street Glory* to Hot 97. I knew in my heart that it could work, but there were people in higher positions that did not see it the same way I felt inside. The show was met with obstacles and opposition that I did not expect, and I had to stay focused and encouraged throughout the process. When you want something bad enough, you will endure whatever pain or delay that comes your way because you will not be satisfied until you accomplish your goal, especially if you feel GOD is with you on the journey. It's like having the best cutman in your corner when fighting for the championship. Your relationships can help you maintain strength in your vision or send you in the opposite

direction. Be sure to surround yourself with positive people who will encourage you and make sure
you don't quit. Thank GOD for my family and my
church family at C.C.C. for believing in me.

Serve to Lead: Servants Are Not Greater Than the
One They Follow

As of today, I'm currently on two FM radio sta-
tions: Hot 97 (NYC) and NGEN Radio 97.1 (Texas), and the podcast show *Sphere of Hip Hop*. I got
to this point by serving or playing for free on so
many other platforms. You see, before GOD will
bless you in public, He needs to be able to trust you
in private. Like my pastor Dr. A.R. Bernard says,
"Private practice determines public performance."

Hard work never goes unnoticed by the people
who can help you. They are willing to give a chance
to someone who is dedicated to what they do. The
gift that GOD has for you can only be expressed
when you work it or use it. Too many people covet
someone else's talent or gift and think, "If I had
that, I would be famous too." The problem with
that thinking is you were not created with that person's talent or gift; so, even if you had it, you still
would not be fulfilled. One thing I have learned
thus far is that seeking GOD brings clarity to how
I see my life.

Before, I would judge everything I saw as if I knew why a person was doing what they were doing. But I have learned to focus more on me, my relationship with the Lord, and the opportunities He has for me.

Life is not as hard as we make it. People often complicate things because of so many distractions, whether it's social media, family, or just not being focused. Trust me, if I remained looking at what other people were doing with their lives, I would have never been able to accomplish the things I have thus far. There are still some dreams I have inside of me, as well as places I believe the Lord has for me to travel. As I shared earlier, when you have been chosen to do something, you don't always know the plans. That is not a bad thing when GOD is the one directing or, as we say, ordering your steps. It all depends on how you look at it. Your vision or perspective on something will determine how far you go, that's why it is so important to surround yourself with people who have purpose and vision for their own lives, because that will challenge you to come up higher.

So many times, I found myself in places where I felt like I didn't belong. But GOD would tell me I did, and I had to adjust how I saw myself. This can be challenging at first, but when you keep surrounding yourself with people who are on a higher level than you, it becomes easier to believe. If I could share a piece of a story from the Word of GOD, a.k.a. the Bible, it would be 1 Samuel 16:14-18. When you get a chance please read it. Briefly, it explains how David was doing what he was created and gifted to do, and people were watching him without him knowing it. In GOD's timing, when the opportunity came, David (having been prepared with the gift GOD placed inside of him) was requested by King Saul. David was then placed in the palace and exposed to a higher way of living and thinking because he was faithful with his gift.

So, the next time you see the spotlight on someone, just know they have been putting in work in the dark and behind the scenes. And if no one else has done what you're trying to do, just remember: "Who said you can't do that?"

Every Minor Setback Sets the Stage for a Major Comeback

Barry J. Clark

I was born on July 20, 1965, to Barry J. Clark Sr. and Thelma Marie Clark. I am the oldest of two living boys. I had an older brother who died at birth. I always remember my mother and father telling me I had an older brother, and I remember feeling abandoned and robbed of the chance to get to know him. I always wished I had someone that could guide and teach me the things I needed to know growing up as opposed to having to be the teacher. I know my parents did the best they could. They had no idea how telling us would impact me or my brother, or that it would foster a sense of abandonment in each of us. I know that being a parent doesn't come with a guide or textbook. Being a parent now myself, I fully understand that you learn by what you see, what you hear, what you're told, and what you might see on TV. It's like baptism by fire. You either learn what to do or what not to do.

I was raised in the projects in Manhattan. Both of my parents worked. My dad as an executive for a shipping company and my mom as an administrative assistant. I always remember feeling fortunate, mainly because I had both parents. Most of my friends came from a single-family household. We traveled, went on family outings, and attended major sporting events. I remember us always going to see Dr. J. at the Nassau Coliseum or Reggie Jackson at Yankee Stadium. I also remember my great-grandfather living in Pittsburgh, Pennsylvania, and going to my first football game at the age of seven, which just so happened to be a playoff game between the Pittsburgh Steelers and the Oakland Raiders. That game turned out to have one of the greatest and most controversial endings to a football game; it is called The Immaculate Reception. Since then, football has been my favorite sport and the Pittsburgh Steelers have been my favorite team.

In 1975, I remember coming home from school one day, and my mother and father sat my brother and I down and shared that we were moving out of the projects into a high-rise building on the Upper West Side. My friends and family would now call us *The Jeffersons*, which was a show on TV based on an African American family that was famous for moving on out from humble beginnings and "moving on up to a deluxe apartment in the sky." I felt sad initially because I had to leave my friends and my school. We really didn't move far, but my father was adamant about us closing that chapter in our lives and starting a new one.

I adjusted quickly to my new surroundings. My building had a doorman, four elevators, a laundry room, and a recreation room. When my friends came to visit, they thought we were rich because of my new surroundings, and I remember feeling extremely uncomfortable with their perception of me and my family. I felt like a square peg trying to fit into a round hole; I was still the same kid that just left the projects. I would later understand that our move didn't change me, it in fact changed my friends and how they treated me and viewed our family. I was always made to feel like I was slightly different based upon being extremely smart and being an excellent reader. I remember being told by my friends that I talked like I was white, which I never liked, nor did I understand. What did white sound like? I had a very difficult time trying to understand why my father gave my brother and I *The New York Times* newspaper to read at such an early age. It was like torture trying to understand what I felt were extremely difficult words to pronounce and spell. But I must say that it was the reason why I developed a college reading level, 12.9+ in the fifth and sixth grades. I always talk about that being one of the greatest teaching methods my brother and I received. There was a saying that was famous when I was growing up. It was: "A mind is a terrible thing to waste." My father was a staunch believer that education, expanding our vocabulary, and enhancing our reading ability and comprehension would be the keys to our success. One of his most famous sayings was, "Your presentation (i.e., how you look and how you conduct yourself) will open and close doors for you in life. But how you speak will either keep you in the room or get you asked to leave."

The Setback

As I discuss with you a time in my life that I feel was the start of a setback period for me and my family, I want you to think of a defining moment or period when things took a turn in your own life.

My father decided to make a career change to support our upward mobility. He decided that he was going to go into law enforcement, which at the time was considered a career defining move. It was also life-changing for my family and I; our lives would go from being what I felt was a glamour story to what would become sort of a horror story. My father went from being a shirt and tie executive to a blue uniform wearing police officer, and ultimately a detective in a very short period of time. I think initially his new career allowed him to feel proud about his professional development and feel a sense of success, as it allowed him to enhance his ability to provide for his family. But I also believe the stressors associated with being a cop and his fractured core beliefs from his upbringing and time in the military (in which he was instilled with a "fight to the death" mantra and a never surrender attitude) kept him in a self-imposed prison. He was paralyzed in his ability to seek and ask for help.

Please, don't get me wrong, I appreciated our upward mobility. It allowed me to be the first person in my neighborhood with DJ equipment, which allowed me to meet and foster new friendships. My allowance went from $25.00 a week to $50.00 a week, which was a lot of money for a kid back in the late 1970's. It made me feel like the big man on campus. It also allowed me to graduate from taking girls out to dinner at Sizzler to being a big spender who wined and dined girls at Beefsteak Charlie's. Those were the days.

The transition from glamour story to horror story was subtle but systematic. We went from a family who always ate dinner together at the same time each day to a family that sat and ate without my father. When we did eat as a family, our discussions at the dinner table were like mini interrogations of who, what, when, where, and how.

I had a hard time adjusting to that new ritual because it thrust me, the oldest child, into my new role as man of the house. My father's pattern changed drastically. It started with the times he would come home, then the times he would spend with me and my brother, and ultimately the time he would spend with my mother. Our house started to overflow with tension. My mother did an amazing job of attempting to maintain a semblance of normalcy for me and my brother, but things were different. There was no masking or pretending that things had and were changing for all of us. As I look back now, none of us were prepared for what was to come.

My mother and father started having minor misunderstandings that escalated into arguments. I remember their arguments being late at night; I guess when he would come in from work. In what seemed like overnight, their arguments grew into shouting matches. I remember how I would put the pillow over my head hoping that would drown out the noise. When that didn't work, I started peeking

Suited For Success, Volume 2

outside of my room door to make sure my mom was ok, or I would go to my brother's room to console him from crying. I couldn't understand what was happening to our family. I found myself feeling like I had to protect my mom and brother, but who was protecting me?!

Just imagine being a teenager thrust into the role of referee and, you won't believe this, hostage negotiator. Yes, just imagine having to negotiate the release of you, your mom, and your brother just to be allowed to go to your in-laws until everyone's feelings calmed down. Then, only a few weeks would go by before we would repeat the process and have to relive the nightmare all over again.

Imagine having to go-between a six-foot-two-inch military man, who at that point was becoming increasingly physically abusive, and a five-foot-one-inch woman. Just imagine being held captive in your own home by the person whom all your life was your hero and your protector.

There was no one to tell. I as the oldest son was bound by a warped and distorted core belief of "What happens in this house, stays in this house." In all actuality, someone needed to know the horrors of what we were experiencing in our home. To the world, my father was a hero cop due

161

to working some extremely high-profile cases in New York at the time, which were the Son of Sam killings and the Larry Davis shootings. To my family and I, he had completely transformed from that hero cop into a villain. Or even better, Mr. Hyde.

The Comeback

You're probably wondering how I came back from all of that? Well, let's just say the road to success is always under construction. My faith and belief in God and my understanding that the universe has to photocopy what you put into it and send it back to you has kept me. I also firmly believe that God doesn't call those whom are equipped, but He equips those whom He calls.

Every situation I previously experienced and described has proven to be the training ground for the work I currently do and the population I've been entrusted to serve.

Who would have thought that most of the experiences I shared in the setback portion of my chapter (from the interrogations at the dinner table, to the hostage negotiations, or having to be a referee) was what I now believe was a preordained part of God's plan for my life? It was almost as if God strategically took me through the battlefield so that I could be prepared to speak to and interact with people on all levels. In my wildest imagination, I never would have thought of how it would serve me so well in my current role as I work with victims of domestic violence by educating them on how to understand the difference between being in a relationship versus being a hostage in a relationship. I also work closely with disenfranchised men and women who are or were connected to the criminal justice system by connecting them to services and teaching them self-esteem building techniques as well as career development and job readiness skills.

I think back to those times at the dinner table when I was being asked a series of rapid-fire questions, and how transferrable that skill has become in my life and career. And how being a referee between my father and mother has helped me mediate truces and disagreements with teenagers as well as young adults who are gang affiliated or at war with rival gangs and neighborhoods. And how being given *The New York Times* newspaper has enhanced and catapulted my ability to not only talk but also to speak, which I feel has been the catalyst to me being asked to be a motivational and keynote speaker at various workshops and events.

We will all experience tragedies in our lives, but they can easily be turned into triumphs. I'm excited to know that my comeback trail has me just starting to scratch the surface of my full potential.

Until we meet again, please be mindful of what you eat but be even more mindful of what you feed yourself.

The Hero Within

Frantz Condé

As far back as I can remember I've always loved heroes. No, I don't mean sandwiches. I'm talking Superman, Batman, Thor, Iron Man, you name it! As long as they had powers and used them for good, it was all gravy. Mom's blanket made the perfect cape, and I would fly off into my imagination to save the world, never suspecting that one day I might have to save myself. Don't get me wrong, my childhood was awesome, especially since I got to play sidekick to my favorite hero of all time, my dad. He was only about 5'8" or so, but to me he was a towering, massive figure that I literally looked up to. In my eyes, he had it all. He was strong, sharp, handsome, well-dressed, battle-tested, well-respected, and he didn't take any crap from anyone. Even his name, Francois Franklin Condé, sounded dashing and important, making me really proud to be his only son. Besides, you had to be tough to be born, raised, and successfully survive in an oppressive Haitian dictatorship; move your wife and two daughters to Chad (where I was born); escape from another oppressive regime; and ultimately, flee to America. Mind you, my parents spoke very little English and lived in constant fear of deportation with very little money. They were trying to survive and feed their children. In spite of all those challenges, they persevered. And with faith in the Creator and a tremendous work ethic, they not only became citizens but they bought a two family home, my dad graduated from college again at 50 (his Haitian degrees weren't recognized), and they still managed to successfully raise a family (first in Crown Heights and eventually in Flatbush, Brooklyn, where I was raised) before and throughout the crack era.

My dad was a man's man and he made you want to become one too. In case you missed it, I'm African-born, Brooklyn-bred, and Haitian-fed. This is usually the part where most people wonder how the heck that happened, and the answer is just as unbelievable as the question itself. We've all heard stories of folks that went from rags to riches, but how many went from riches to rags while securing the bag? I know, enough with the suspense already. So here goes my true confession: I'm quite literally the real-life *Coming to America* story, minus the rose bearers. Yes, THAT *Coming to America*! Back when Haiti was still prosperous economically, one of its most prominent attorneys, professors, philosophers, and businessmen was selected to represent the country as an ambassadorial diplomat to Chad which had recently won its independence. That man was my late uncle, The Honorable Lionel Lubin of Les Cayes. After developing a fantastic relationship with the Chadian government, he was able to successfully relocate his entire family there, including my parents and two older sisters who were all born in Haiti. Having worked as educators, my parents were granted a lucrative government contract to teach with the blessing of the president, who was more so like a king than anything and would later become my godfather. That's right, I was literally baptized by an actual king, President Tombalbaye of the Sará tribe... Wakanda forever.

As guests of the royal presidential family, we were afforded all of the luxuries that came with it: mansions, cars, limousines, chauffeurs, private security, maids, personal chefs, servants, you name it! Of course, as a newborn, I was too young to remember any of that but for those relatives that do, membership definitely had its privileges. For as long as he was in power, we were living large. And had everything gone according to plan, today I would be speaking French, Arabic, several African dialects, and I would no doubt be a head of state as was my godfather's desire and proclamation. Before I could even walk, it seemed like my life was set. But, life has a funny way of resetting the stage when you least expect it. What was once a dream would soon become a nightmare when rival tribes and longtime enemies violently took over the government, assassinated my godfather, threw my uncle in jail, and were now after my family, especially me. Although I was born there, I was not necessarily considered a native (an indigenous African) even though both my parents are black. To the other tribes, we were foreigners trying to take over their country, so we had to be dealt with accordingly.

Almost overnight, we went from being guests of the royal family to fugitives of the government. We literally had to flee for our lives and we narrowly escaped to nearby Cameroon. With unwavering faith in God, my dad was able to throw on his cape and save his family from certain death. Going back to Haiti was no longer an option since we might be considered spies, which also meant certain death or imprisonment in a cruel dictatorship. My dad's only option was to either stay in Cameroon or move to France or Canada with whatever resources and documents we were able to salvage. What happened next was God working and fate in action. My paternal uncle, the late great Amaury Condé, had recently migrated to America and convinced my dad to stay with him until he could figure out his next move. Little did we know, America would become our new home. Having barely escaped from Chad before I could even walk, I became severely ill en route to America and once again I almost lost my life.

Luckily for me, God had something else in mind. Although I didn't know it then, looking back has taught me that we are created for greatness and there is a king in all of us waiting to be born. We are conceived as princes but programmed to be peasants. And if we're not careful, we can be stripped of our crowns. Nonetheless, as long as we're alive, we can fight for our calling, our kingdom, and our destiny through faith, hard work, determination, and discipline. We all must face our fears. And we will inevitably go through crap, but it is up to us to overcome that crap by first overcoming ourselves. We must use negativity as fertilizer for our goals and fuel for our dreams.

Speaking of dreams, my folks originally had no plans of staying in America and pursuing the American dream, especially after living the type of life that most Americans only dream of. But, with limited options and depleting resources, they decided to make the best of their situation until they could create their own. That meant that they would literally be starting all over again from ground zero since in this country their education, experience, and diplomatic relationships meant nothing, not to mention they barely spoke English. Nonetheless, against all odds and with only the help of my uncle (who was raising a family of his own), they persevered and never gave up. Eventually, they found a way.

Going from lavish living to initially working factory jobs was a hard pill to swallow, but pride doesn't pay the bills. Scraping together every penny while taking care of me and my two sisters, eventually we were able to move out of my uncle's place and into our first apartment at 235 Midwood Street in Crown Heights, Brooklyn. That's where my childhood began and some of my fondest memories were created. When my maternal uncle, Rulx Lubin (a businessman as well as a priest), decided to open up Flatbush Preschool, my parents left their factory slave wages and joined his staff as educators. They became my first teachers both at home and in school. Aside from living in a great neighborhood community, I absolutely loved learning and couldn't wait for my dad to get home from work so I could fetch his slippers and he could help me with my homework. Believe it or not, that was my very first job and it paid a whopping $1 per week. That might not seem like a lot now, but to a third grader back in the day, it was everything. It was also my first lesson in finance. I still remember saving a dollar every week until I had enough to buy my first music album, *Thriller*, by my favorite artist, Michael Jackson! I still have that album to this day. And every time I play it, I remember the man who gave me the patience and discipline to make it possible and my wonderful Mom who took me to the record store and was so proud of me for saving up and practicing delayed gratification. Of course, I also had to get the grades and earn it both academically and monetarily. I honestly believe this is a lost art and one we need to bring back to our community. Everything in life must be earned; the universe frowns upon bargains and no one truly respects or appreciates what they can get for free.

Leading by example, my parents somehow also managed to put us through private school at Holy Cross for three years before we eventually moved to Flatbush. We were the first people of color in that neighborhood and the only ones to own a home, which still amazes me to this day and demonstrates that when you have a dream and the faith to pursue it, with God, you will eventually attain it. I was very fortunate to have both parents, especially in the crack cocaine era. I love and respect my parents deeply, and I thank God that my mom is still with me while my dad watches over me. I still remember how he used to brag about me to his friends and relatives and had high hopes of me becoming a doctor, which I later found out was his unfulfilled dream. I cherished every minute of him helping me with my homework, taking me to the barbershop, showing me how to tie a tie, and even how to get out of a headlock. There was literally nothing he wouldn't do for us, and I always felt safe, valued, and validated whenever I was fortunate enough to be in his presence. To me, he was invincible and could do no wrong. But, I was wrong, and now he's gone. I feel his eternal presence even now while emotional raindrops drip through my mind, pierce my heart, and suffocate my soul, longing for days of yesterday. I lost my hero on March 2, 2011. But in many ways, I lost him long before that. And eventually, I lost myself too. Without warning, another major shift in our family dynamic was about to take place, and things would never be the same again. I had only heard rumors about my three other sisters on my dad's side, but I had no connection to them since they lived in Haiti. I had never been to Haiti and barely spoke Creole. Two of them had come to live with us now that we had a home of our own and enough space to accommodate them, or so we believed.

It's hard to pinpoint exactly when my relationship with my dad began to deteriorate, but I honestly believe he felt guilty about not being there for them and wanted to make up for lost time. I would experience his powerful absence firsthand. I wish I could really go into detail, but one chapter alone wouldn't do it justice. Suffice it to say, what used to be words of encouragement and upliftment became constant discouragement and harsh criticism. What used to be spirited trips to the barbershop became quiet walks of desperation. What used to be homework help became, "I'm busy, do it yourself." What used to be quality time became no time at all, except for constant criticism, mockery, and flat out looks of utter disgust. Almost overnight, I was abandoned in my own home, and what was once my greatest source of power became my greatest source of pain.

Outside of basic necessities, I could no longer count on my dad for anything and in a world where being both African and Haitian was looked down upon, I was literally left to fend for myself. I used to hang on his every word, but now his every word hung me, and I was choking and gasping for breath. I went from courageous to cowardice and from fighter to fearful. Inside, I was dying and did everything I could to make up for whatever sin I must've committed to cause my hero to hate me, but to no avail. I felt abandoned, worthless, and I even thought about ending it all. Had it not been for the voice of God within me, I would be a distant memory. Words are powerful; they can give life or take it away. So be careful who you listen to, especially when talking to yourself. Although my dad was there physically, he was pretty much MIA when I needed him the most.

Ironically, what I lost mentally and emotionally, I began to gain and reclaim spiritually. That's where my new Father-son relationship transformation began. Not with my dad's words, but with the Word. I stopped listening to and believing my dad's toxic words and started believing in the words of my Creator and His beloved Son. I found out that the Word said I was the son of a King, a mighty conqueror and heir to the throne of glory. I found out that I could build myself into my true self with the help of the Holy Spirit. To be clear, I'm not religious, I just found out the truth for myself and built my life around that. Yes, life can be painful, and we can be tempted to give up and give in, but that's the time to dig deep and go within. I started speaking what I wanted instead of what I had. I learned to lead by example and replace sadness with service and bitterness with kindness. I learned to love myself by going to and submitting to the source of love so that I could properly love others. I learned to ask five major questions that would forever change my life and to let my heavenly Father answer them. Those questions were:

1. Who am I?
2. Where am I from?
3. Why am I here?
4. What am I capable of?
5. Where am I going?

As a result of asking those questions, I've been able to discover my true inner self as well as my true calling—using my gifts, talents, abilities, character, integrity, and personality to lead people to their Source through Christ which strengthens me. Today, I'm the founding president and CEO of Condé & Associates, Condé Global, and Condé Global Entertainment. I have a dual master's degree in education, and I am an aspiring honorary doctoral candidate at Morehouse College. I'm pursuing my passions as a global entrepreneur, educator, empowerment speaker, and entertainer. I'm also in the process of becoming the world's greatest visionary artîste and creative storyteller par excellence. But most importantly, I'm overcoming my old self to become my true self. And guess what, Champ? So can you! Your destiny is calling, don't let it go to voicemail! Overcome to become and discover the hero within!

Control

Garry Smalley

"Play the cards you were dealt." "If given lemons make lemonade." Those are both clichés that we hear throughout our lives, but what do these sayings really mean and how can they help us overcome the hassles and stressors we face on a daily basis? I can tell you that in my 42 years of living, a few things will always hold true. The first is, life is not always fair. The second is, things will not always turn out how you expect or plan. The third is simple, the best way to succeed is to control what is within your power to control. I have started businesses that have not been successful, I have had an unsuccessful marriage, and I have come close to bankruptcy. Failure can be embarrassing and discouraging; however, if you change your perception, it can also be an empowering and enlightening learning tool.

The truth is there is no magic formula to success; however, there is a formula to increase your chances for success. I mentioned earlier about controlling the things you can control, and the one thing you can control is yourself. You can control your focus, preparation, planning, attitude, dedication, and commitment. Many people say they want success, but without the work which includes everything I just mentioned, they fall short of the goal. Once the going gets tough they drop the ball, they make excuses, and they quit, not knowing that their big break is literally one or two handshakes or conversations away. You must always plan to succeed and if you don't reach the level of success you desire, it is important to be able to look at yourself in the mirror and with honesty say, "I did all I could to make this a success." If you can't say that, you will always question yourself. "Did I really do enough to succeed? Maybe I…"

I want to share with you some of my life experiences which include both successes and failures. In addition, I will share insight into the valuable lessons I was taught. I'll begin with F.O.C.U.S. And no, I'm not talking about the ability to apply your dedicated brain energy to a situation, idea, or solution. F.O.C.U.S. was the first company that I attempted to create. F.O.C.U.S. stands for Family Organization Coming Under Structure. It consisted of cousins and uncles looking to earn money in real estate by purchasing homes with renovation needs. The goal was to fix up and flip those properties for a profit. Our target region was where we all were living at the time; the Norfolk and Tidewater, Virginia, area. It seemed like a no-brainer because my uncles were carpenters and electricians, my cousins and I were just out of college, and we all knew that real estate was the best way to build generational wealth. We got incorporated, we had meetings, and we created business cards. Ironically though, we lacked focus. In our meetings, we would spend our time talking about all kinds of business ideas from opening the first White Castle in the Tidewater area to creating a F.O.C.U.S. clothing line. Although those were some great discussions, our meetings were very unproductive. Truthfully, we needed to seek assistance from someone that had successfully done what we were trying to do. That was a huge oversight, and because of that eight months passed and we found ourselves in the same place we were in when I first proposed the idea.

We never raised much money and we never spoke to a mortgage broker. Heck, we never did a walkthrough on a property. Eventually, members began finding excuses to not come to meetings and within a year we were no longer meeting.

What was the lesson? A great idea is really nothing if you don't have a plan. Had we outlined a plan and sought help from an expert in the early stages so that we could properly develop the idea, we would be real estate moguls today. Remember that as long as you learn the lesson it is not failure. What could we have controlled to increase our chances of success? Focusing on the goal—property flipping. When in a group it can be easy to get sidetracked. Write down the agenda for every meeting and stick to it. Secondly, seek advice from a professional that has succeeded in what you are seeking to accomplish.

A positive mental attitude, also known as PMA, can take you far in life. During my insurance career, I spent a great deal of time at a top auto insurance company. I worked my way up from customer service to Affinity program manager, and by the time I parted ways my territory was the entire United States. The road to my success was not easy. I faced several situations that if I had allowed them to they would have discouraged me, made me disgruntled, or both. By controlling what I can control, which is my attitude, I was able to overcome and make myself highly successful within the company.

I applied for a supervisory position and as a part of that process I was partnered with a very seasoned and successful supervisor. My idea of how I would like to manage a team and the supervisory style of the supervisor-mentor I was paired with was vastly different. Throughout my work career, I was a firm believer in the concept of "Praise in public and chastise in private." However, my supervisor-mentor believed in praising and chastising in public. Many times, I would watch as the supervisor-mentor would scream and yell at people in front of their peers or send degrading emails about a person's performance to the entire team. I just couldn't and wouldn't buy into that approach to supervising, so we bumped heads.

There was a situation where a person was having issues meeting their goals. That person was historically excellent in their job performance. After speaking to the person, I realized that there were several areas that had changed in the employee's personal life that may have contributed to her lack of performance and inability to hit her goals. I disclosed that information to the supervisor and she used it in a way that I felt was unfair. The employee, under stress from work and stress in her personal life, was given a warning that if goals were not hit in 30 days she would be terminated. I truly felt it was unfair because of that employee's longevity with the company and her prior success. I spoke up on behalf of that person. The supervisor-mentor saw that as me challenging authority and gave me a very bad review. She went so far as to say that I didn't have a backbone and I was unfit for management.

There were eight of us in that program and they had seven positions available for supervisors. Because of that review, I was not allowed to interview and was told by my direct supervisor that I should, "Go back to underwriting and lose yourself." I remember thinking, "Well, I can go complain to human resources or I can be angry about the process and make excuses because of the person I was partnered with." It did upset me, but I knew I needed to control what I could control and that was me and my attitude about the situation. I went back to underwriting. I continued to show my value while an underwriter and waited for the next opportunity. I chose to return to underwriting with a positive mental attitude and within six months a new position became available. It was a high-profile position requiring 80 percent travel and was only being offered to supervisors and above. My underwriting supervisor approached me one day and said "Garry, you're very outgoing.

You think outside of the box. Why don't you apply for this position? I know it may be a longshot, but I will put a word in for you so that they waive the requirement of you being a supervisor. Technically you're a leader in the underwriting department anyway."

What did I have to lose? So, I applied for the position. There was a pre-assignment that needed to be completed and turned in on the day of the interview. I spent two weekends preparing. I created a PowerPoint and a marketing strategy, and I made sure that I understood the math required for the position. There were eight people that interviewed for the position, all supervisors and managers. I was the ninth and last interviewee, and because I didn't have the title like those interviewing before me, it felt like I had no chance. In spite of how it felt, I put in the work, I planned, I was positive, and I went into that interview prepared. I walked in with my slides and was told the PowerPoint projector was down. Because I was prepared, I had printed out my slides. And because I had rehearsed my interview so much, I actually set my laptop in front of the interviewer and went through the presentation where each slide was timed so the slides changed on their own. At the end of the interview, the interviewer said, "Wow, that was creative!"

At that company, the protocol was to notify the person who is receiving the position last and to notify all the interviewees who are not receiving the position first. My interview was at 2:30 p.m. and by 3:00 p.m. I was being called back downstairs to meet with the interviewer. In my mind, I knew I did not receive the position, but I remained positive. To my surprise, the interviewer said, and I quote, "This is not protocol, but I am telling you that you received the position before I'm telling anyone they did not receive it." I couldn't believe it! That high profile position where I would be negotiating deals with university presidents on behalf of the insurance company was mine. Later I found out that of all the interviewees, I was the most prepared by far and it showed. What was the lesson? In spite of what happened in my attempts to be a supervisor, I remained positive and continued to show my value. I was provided an opportunity to take my career beyond the normal insurance career path. My desire to succeed couldn't stop at being offered this new position. I had to plan and prepare to be successful in the new role.

Although you plan and are dedicated, things will not always turn out how you expect. Therefore, you must be flexible. Then because you have a plan or blueprint, you are able to maneuver and take advantage of opportunities that come your way. When I left the insurance company to start my own consulting business, my goal was to assist universities with renegotiating their programs with insurance carriers. I mean, I had all of the contacts and the knowledge. Planning the business was a great learning experience, but I still needed to make income while the business got off the ground. So, I began teaching insurance licensing classes on evenings and weekends while I grew my consulting company during the day. It was long hours and little pay, but another opportunity was birthed from the consulting company and it forever changed my life. Consulting with universities became a small part of my company's revenue and assisting former students with opening their own insurance agencies became a huge revenue stream.

Think about it. I could teach them all they needed to know about insurance to pass the licensing exam and then they would come right back to me and say, "Hey, can you help me open my own insurance agency or insurance brokerage?" I did not see that opportunity coming, but I was able to take full advantage of it. I consulted with people from a variety of races, age groups, and financial backgrounds to guide them through the process of opening and running successful insurance agencies.

Using the same skills of focusing, planning, and preparing that I learned through my professional career, I was able to share my knowledge with those agency owners. What is the lesson? Control what you can control! Because I had a plan and understood my time commitment to consulting with universities, I was able to easily augment my plan to include agency consulting.

I know that life will not always be fair, and even when you apply the concept of controlling what is in your power to control you may not have the level of success you desire. In spite of that, you should always be able to look in the mirror and say, "I gave it my all. I did all I could to be successful." And if you don't meet the level of success you expected, remember that it is not a failure if you learn the lesson.

Grow Your Relationships and You Will Grow!

Larry Scott Blackmon

Relationship development is a challenge because proper relationship cultivation is something that is rarely taught, particularly in communities of color. Many of us have probably destroyed more relationships than we've cultivated, and I am certainly no different. That said, believe me, my success has been in large part due to relationship development. I strongly encourage you to grow your relationships.

Now let me start by saying that unfortunately, I had a late start on writing my chapter for this book for a number of reasons, so I am jeopardizing my relationship with Mr. Kersey! That said, all good things come in due time and I hope that the messages I deliver in this chapter resonate with you.

Relationships matter. Throughout my career I've been blessed to have relationships with individuals that I've helped and those who have helped me on my journey to success. The interesting thing about relationships is that there are positive and negative benefits to building them. The challenge and the question for the ages is: how do you effectively quantify the value of a relationship?

In my eyes, the easiest way to begin to understand the value of a relationship is by actually looking at it through the rearview mirror if you will. Once a relationship has expired, one recognizes the value that was there (or lack thereof). I certainly have had my share of burned bridges throughout my career and my share of regrets as it relates to people who I wanted to connect with that ultimately moved on to great positions and careers. I regret that one transaction with them that cost me in the long run. As a result, in this chapter I am going to share tips with you to help you grow and understand the power and the value of a relationship. Let's dive right into this by defining relationships.

What Is a Relationship?

I was fortunate enough to have attended a course on executive leadership at the John F. Kennedy School of Government at Harvard University. About five percent of what I'm sharing with you originates from that course. Dr. Marshall Ganz, the professor of the course, was one of the most amazing instructors I've ever had in my career as he defined relationships in a manner that I had never heard before.

So, with that said, how does one define relationships? A relationship is a connection that you make with someone. Relationships are an exchange. Relationships are about that one moment of truth that exists. In the moment of truth, or at a time of great need, having that special relationship can bring clarity and can even help you get your questions answered. Can I count on you to deliver?

I've been blessed throughout my career. Believe it or not, I have delivered for people in one way or another. Just recently, I was in an introductory meeting with a colleague at my office when I was interrupted by a tenant leader in the neighborhood who called and said, "Mr. Blackmon, I don't have gas coming into three of my buildings. Can you help me?" My first thought was, "Why are you calling me when the office of the city council member is directly across the street from your building?" But due to understanding the relationship value, understanding that this person needed help immediately, and understanding that she probably felt like there was one person she can go to for help, I told her without hesitation that I would provide assistance immediately. I sent a message to someone who worked in the mayor's office at City Hall who then forwarded information to the public housing authority, which acted expeditiously to resolve the issue.

Relationships are about cultivation. One of the frustrating views I find is that people believe that they are not supposed to put anything into building a relationship with someone. That in no way means that you need to be overly friendly. Relationships are like plants in that you have to plant a seed with someone. You have to respect that seed. You have to water it, nurture it, and grow it over time. You would not overwater your plants and at the same time you do not want to over saturate your relationship with someone. Just because you have access to that person doesn't mean that person is always accessible. One needs to know the balance between being a friend and becoming a burden.

Respect Their Authority

As a person of color, I am naturally paranoid. I drive a nice car and I'm especially paranoid when I am pulled over by the police. I respect the authority of the officer I am engaged with at that time. That same respect translates to my place of work and how I engage with my colleagues. While I am by no means in a secure position forever, thankfully because of my work and the fact that I have delivered for our company, I am in a good position with many of my colleagues.

If someone is in a position of power, naturally there are those who try to extract some of that power for their benefit. Power takes many forms: accessibility, financial responsibility, influence, and more. Some say that relationship building is about extraction because in a relationship one party may look to extract something from the other. Usually, one of the two are in a position of power or a position of influence. The unfortunate side to this is when someone feels as though they need to "go around you" to get what they need. I have had that happen to me on more than one occasion and I implore you that going around someone and usurping their authority, particularly as it relates to ethnic lines or ethnic background, is extraordinarily dangerous and can instantly lead to relationship destruction. I will never forget how I felt years ago when, while working for an elected official, I engaged a visitor to the office who was Jewish. I was asked pointblank if I was Jewish and when I said, "No," he replied, "Well, I'm sorry, I really don't want to deal with you. I'd like to talk to someone else." The state director at the time, after hearing this story about the person who was at the reception desk, told me, "You tell him that if he does not talk to you, he will not talk to anyone in this office." I gladly conveyed that message. To this day, I hold my former colleague in the highest regard. It takes courage to not play along racial lines in our relationships. Attempting to go around someone is an instant death knell for any relationship you attempt to build.

Avoid the "Once a Year Trap"

There are certain times where it's alright to only contact someone once a year. Unless you're from another planet, you have a birthday once a year. Most holidays only come around once a year. But what should not happen is relationship cultivating taking place only once a year. There are many people who have annual events and the only time they conduct outreach to try to solicit support is annually when that event comes back around.

As I mentioned earlier, relationship building is all about cultivation. If you are only talking to someone because you need something, chances are the person in control knows that and will only grant that wish to people they've engaged with throughout the year. I call it the "once a year trap." Working at a food company, I know the one time of year that I'm going to hear from people—Thanksgiving. That is when community residents and leaders are looking for turkeys to be donated. I literally reject hundreds of people who ask for free turkeys at that time of year.

While that is no means because of personal preference, there are individuals who stand with the company and who work with us, so quite naturally those people should be rewarded for the fact that they stood and worked with us to make things happen. I cultivate relationships by avoiding the trap and making sure that I reach out to people periodically just to say hello. I encourage you to work relationships and ensure that they extend far beyond the "once a year trap."

Value One-on-One Meetings

There are different relational tactics that I am mentioning, but probably out of all of them, the one-on-one meeting is extremely important. As I learned in my executive leadership course at Harvard University, the primary purpose of the one-on-one meeting is to build a relationship out of which further involvement in your goal or the organization may develop. The one-on-one meeting is successful if it ends with a commitment to a next step, which may include another meeting. One-on-

one meetings allow time for two people to discover that they may have shared common interests. You reveal how much you learn about each other and how well you can establish a rapport in a relatively short time.

I have found that there are certain unwritten rules to one-on-one meetings, and I would like to share a few of them. First, one should be mindful of the time of day that you request the meeting. Generally, I try to meet with people as early in the day as possible, mostly over coffee or tea. Mornings are unimpacted by the day's incidents. Usually by the afternoon, people are preparing to go home or preparing for their evening's activities, and late day meetings pull people from their schedules. I'd much rather have their attention in the morning.

Secondly, if you ask for an in-person meeting with someone, it is critically important that you show up on time. There is nothing worse than being late for a meeting that you requested. Arriving on time means that you should arrive early, before your guest, and be there waiting to receive the other party. The third tip that I would like to share is that if you are meeting with someone over food, try to be mindful of your manners during the meeting. I once had a dinner meeting with a prospective sponsor at a seafood restaurant. While eating the lobster, this person proceeded to forgo the metal shell cracker and instead she cracked the lobster shell with her teeth as if it were a crab! I had never seen anything like that before and I have never seen anything like that since. Now my memory of the meeting is not about the content, but of the visual of someone trying to extract every morsel of lobster meat out of the shell with their teeth. Be mindful of your manners at the table and if necessary, review proper table manners prior to meeting.

The final note about the one-on-one meeting that I will share is somewhat controversial. If you ask for a one-on-one meeting and that meeting is at a restaurant, you should always pay the bill. Do not allow your guest to split the bill for a meeting that they did not request. You asked, they agreed; the least you can do is cover the cost as a sign of appreciation.

Bump What You Heard

Unless you are a newborn child, we all have reputations that have developed over the course of our lives. Some reputations are more positive than others. It is my view that when attempting to build a relationship with someone, you should always go in with the understanding that the person you are trying to work with should have a clean slate in your mind. It's very hard to build relationships with someone in today's world. We live in a world where before you even meet with the person, you can Google search to find out whatever information has been posted online about them. More often than not, reviews, comments, and posts put up online do not accurately represent exactly who that person may be in person. I always try to avoid the urge to search for someone or to look something up online prior to meeting someone in person. The reality for me—and I share this with you—is that whatever their past has been that is by no means an indicator of what their future relationship with me could become. So "bump what you heard" (forget what you heard) as they say in Harlem. Go into a new relationship with a clean slate.

Humans are very judgmental and relationship building is about an understanding between two people. It's very hard to have an understanding if you prejudge someone before you had an opportunity to meet them for yourself. Going in with a completely clean slate, a positive outlook, and a willingness to build will lead to a positive outcome.

How You Hang Up Matters

How do you manage adversity if you are the receiver of some type of rejection? Whether it is a letter of rejection, a phone call rejection, or an in-person rejection, how an individual manages adversity says a lot about that individual. Throughout my career, I've always been seen as a resource to people or an individual that people seek out for assistance with employment. I'm not a big fan of the referral because some people take it for granted and do not appreciate what it takes to build relationships. When things do not work out, how you hang up matters. Here's a quick story to prove that point.

One day, the son of a friend called and asked for assistance with finding employment. After opening the door and creating an opportunity, the individual was interviewed and made it to the second phone call interview to move the process along. After receiving some disappointing news (he wasn't going to be hired) about his background check, my referral slammed the phone down on my colleague. To say that I was disappointed is an understatement. How you hang up the phone matters for several reasons.

First, it shows the person that you are appreciative of their efforts. Slamming the phone down or being unprofessional has the dual effect of not only representing you in a negative light, it may impact the referrer's ability to ever try to place anyone else in a position again.

Secondly how you hang up the phone conveys your ability to manage disappointment. While I'm using the metaphor of hanging up the phone, the reality is that in relationships we are all faced with challenges in difficult times. Some people handle adversity easier than others, but the fact remains that how you deal with adversity and how you deal with negativity matters. Always keep in mind that people are watching you and having an even-keeled personality is helpful. Hang up the phone in the same manner you pick it up—pleasantly.

Make Someone Remember You

So after you've had your one-on-one meeting, after you've respectfully disengaged, and after you've done everything that I've suggested in this chapter, the last thing that you need to focus on in order to make relationships matter is to ensure that the person remembers you. I have employed different methods of doing so and in today's technologically advanced and fast-paced world, you need to employ tried and true techniques that make you stand out. Please consider the following.

Follow up with a thank you phone call. Unless laws prohibit, send someone a thank you gift. Send an old-fashioned letter that you typed on your own stationary. Even better, send someone a handwritten thank you note.

There are many ways that you can make yourself stand out. I try to send someone a thank you letter whenever I receive one of their business cards. I also catalog emails and have a database for phone calls that I need to return. Given technological advancements, there is absolutely no reason why following up with someone should not occur. This is a "dog eat dog" society, and the challenge and goal of separating yourself from the rest should be accomplished by making someone remember you, obviously for something positive.

Old relationships are due to be renewed and new relationships need to be developed in order for us to succeed as individuals and as a community. There's an old saying, "No man is an island unto himself." There is value in relationships but only if they are cultivated in the appropriate manner.

Overcoming the challenges that we face is a daunting task. But, with relationships that matter and with a network that is strong and properly cultivated, there are very few challenges that are insurmountable. With the help of your relationships, you will be properly suited for success.

Cheated but Not Defeated: You Must Fail in Order to Prevail!

Norman Grayson

"Daddy, please don't leave!" Words uttered by a three-year-old boy knee-high to a grasshopper, too young to gauge the rationale between two consenting adults as he stood at the door. The malefactor, through the eyes of the child, was his dad (an accountant by day and an entertainer by night) who expressed to his female counterpart, Kathryn (a mother by day, an educator throughout the day, a barmaid, a wife, and a mother again by night), that entertaining, traveling, and meeting people was his goal in life. Maybe it didn't mean much to him at the time. He probably convinced himself that Katie would be just fine because she had help from Audrey, who was juggling sister-mother responsibilities in exchange for her youth. Dennis and Denise were the 10-year-old twins, tier two support just in case the big sister bus broke down. The little boy at the door, Norman Jr., he would deal with later when he was old enough to understand. Realistically, it had to be difficult to make that choice to leave your family and to do so unwaveringly no matter how painful. Kathryn (a.k.a. Mrs. Katie) made Norman Sr. perfectly aware that she loved him and would not interfere with his dreams. She said pointedly, "But be clear, as soon as that door closes behind you, everything changes, including the lock and key."

My mother never talked sideways about my father to me nor blamed him for their separation which ultimately led to divorce. But she was also a straight shooter, so if you weren't prepared to hear HER truth, then stay quiet. I spoke to my dad in spurts during my childhood through a combination of letters and phone calls that we took turns initiating. At 12 years young, I graduated to a visit! He flew me out to California for 10 wonderful days after convincing Katie to put me on a 747 solo flight non-stop to Los Angeles.

After that trip, dialogue between the two of us remained consistent well into my 20's. I found myself attempting to retrieve the lost years. After all, he did miss all of my "firsts" and an explanation was warranted. Just like my mom, he never gave an impression that she was the reason why it didn't work. So, due to my rationale, I made myself the reason for their split. Since they were not blaming each other, maybe the problem was that they didn't agree on bringing me into the picture! I mean, before I came on the set the twins were the youngest at 10 years old and to start fresh with another baby was probably not in the plan. Then I questioned and doubted, making up scenarios that had no validation or truth to them. Like, maybe I was an accident from improper birth control precautions and a result of being "in the moment." It was difficult to think straight. Those were just some of the scenarios that ran through my head, but when multiplied by 365 days, then times that number by 17 years, all you end up with is a ball of confusion in the mind of a young black man trying to make sense of it all.

On another visit, at an age just south of 25, he and I took a weekend road trip from Los Angeles to Mexico. During that journey we had Q&A time. We each shared a lot of information about ourselves and knowing things about him made me understand what made me tick. Although there was a lot that I had learned, there was a lot that I was not privy to.

At the age of 25, when we should have been sitting down together sharing beers and tears about the past, present, and future, I was preparing his

obituary and picking out his clothes for crema-
tion. It felt like he was leaving me again, but for
good this time, with questions that only maturity respected. It was his choice not to disclose his
sickness, and I had to respect that. So, in March
of 1995, while my wife was carrying our first child
and son, I was burying my dad twice—deep inside
the earth and deep inside of myself.

I was too ashamed to share the ordeal in detail. I even kept it from my brother who looked up
to our dad. My brother passed away about eight
years thereafter from cancer while my wife was
pregnant with our second child and first daughter.
So here it was, two births, two deaths, and when
my wife was pregnant with our third child and second daughter, I was convinced that the third death
was going to be me. Why? I was overweight and
being a diabetic didn't help.

As time passed, I confided in Bishop and
Overseer Clarence V. Keaton and Pastor Spencer
Wright, both from The True Worship Church
Worldwide Ministries, regarding the turmoil within. They gave council on the matter, totally unaware
of the challenges they themselves were facing with
their health. They each passed away less than two
years apart. Those men were my mentors and father figures to me. Within a span of 15 years, all

of those men, between the ages of 35 and 56, went home to glory. I felt cheated due to not having a male mentor to help me become a man, brother, father, and leader. I had no male role model to till the ground in my life, no rite of passage ceremony, only tears of what could have and should have been. I even reached out to other prominent men that were established in their lives to mentor me, only to be told that they "did not have the time." At my lowest state is when it hit me. I had to work on becoming the person that I always wanted in my life!

In times of despair, some of the greatest moments are born. You're shown that sometimes things have to fall apart before they can fall into place. When I was meditating on what point of view I needed to share with you, I first had to define what type of success I wanted to "suit" you with. In this sense, the word suited in *Suited for Success* is interchangeable with prepared, repaired, or any other word that defines how you choose to identify with success. And what better angle to show than that which says that success is birthed from what we perceive as failures, specifically ones stemming from situations beyond our control.

The analogy of the caterpillar morphing into a butterfly is deeper than you can imagine. Although it is important to know that the caterpillar, after spending time in a cocoon, becomes this beautiful, colorful flying creation in nature, it's even more important to understand that after the transformation has taken place, never again do you see the butterfly in the presence of caterpillars. The butterfly has a new role that involves learning to be a butterfly by being in the presence of other butterflies. This is known as disassociation after development. Once development has taken place, there is no need to function as a butterfly with caterpillar tendencies. So, once your mental metamorphosis takes place, there is no reason to reside in non-progressive logic that will keep you in bondage. In order to appreciate the development of a new and improved me, I had to disassociate from that mindset by disconnecting from entities that ignite confusion.

We often conceptualize failure and quitting as being synonymous. Nothing can be further from the truth. Visualize success to be the athlete that you're striving to become, and failure is the life coach that corrects and coaches you to be better, adjusts your strategies, and changes your form. Failure is also the teacher that challenges you to step up your research skills and fine tune your process in order to function at optimum performance.

We can feel justified in saying why certain things happened to us, but honesty will separate the facts from the truth that there is no moral victory in blaming. Maybe you didn't grow up with the finer things in life and tragedy shadowed you through the swamp of shortcomings, but I submit to you that even if you feel cheated, you are not defeated. In *Suited for Success, Vol. 1*, I took for a title "Till Faith No Longer Possesses Parameters" meaning operate in what you know no matter how small and it will eventually expand without measure.

Everyone celebrates success differently. But whether it's financial, spiritual, physical, graduating from a learning institution, achieving an athletic accomplishment, or a job promotion outer excellence requires an inner hunger to excel. Levels of success require failure, hunger, and training. Be aware that every parishioner's "burning testimony" or "rags to riches" story overcame mountains of mental stumbling blocks to achieve next level results, only to be tested again on the new level that awaits. Failure, hunger, and training are a constant on this road. With the passing of my father, brother, bishop, and pastor, I thought that my development with the help of men that mattered most to me was all but lost, but God made them all a part of me!

When addressing the hand that life has dealt me and everything that I felt I had lost, the one thing that helped me and I'm certain will help you is to never lose your ability to think or utilize your mind. Don't allow people to tell you that talking to yourself is crazy. Give yourself positive reminders through prayers, quotes, Scriptures, and affirmations. I have two friends at work, and one of them always says that it's not always about doing what one wants to do because natural things and spiritual things have a protocol that must be followed. The other friend has a message on her writing board that reads: "Nothing changes if nothing changes."

A quote that I created to keep me on track states, *Evaluate what yesterdays you convey to the you of today in case tomorrow's you is eavesdropping.* In other words, be deliberate in your thoughts daily because they can affect your future decision-making. I would like to share these four points with you as this chapter comes to a close.

1 - Define your hunger.

In the Bible, Genesis 25:24-34 tells the story of twin brothers named Esau and Jacob. In the story, one brother's natural temporal hunger betrays him and he loses his inheritance, position, and birthright to his twin brother who chose to fulfill his spiritual hunger (which according to Scripture began in their mothers' womb). Make sure that your spiritual hunger supersedes your natural hunger. Don't allow the desires of your flesh to dictate what success entails. Accept nothing without examination but also reject nothing without consideration. If something is truly a passion or a desire, obtaining it is nonnegotiable.

2 - Guard your mind.

Any manifestation of a person's ability to accomplish anything in life already exists in their mind as being doable. Whether it's "anything is possible" or "nothing is impossible," the common denominator is still infinity. Elevating your mind is an exit from a prison with no key, no door, and no windows. And pretty much, like the body, strength and growth is the reward. Read as much as you can. The mind is a sponge and absorbs knowledge subconsciously, unsealing the lips of objectiveness to question that which you were programmed not to ask yourself. Spend time in prayer or meditation. Use quiet time to focus on changing your vibration to a frequency that is in tune with the universe. When it seems like you're straying off the right path, your spirit will bring you back into alignment, recognizing the voice of reason or the God within you.

3 - Perceive failure differently.

Success accomplished at any level will testify that failure is a part of the growth process. To cease trying is to cease growing; furthermore, there are people that God has prepared for you to be able to help. So, when failure becomes the excuse to quit, the trajectory of your future changes. But by staying the course and learning from failing, preparation will soon connect to opportunity. How we define failure will determine our worthiness for success, and success without stories of failure come off as bragging.

4 - Develop an acronym to govern your direction.

Here's an example that you can use as a template and then you can prepare one that best suits you.

T - Transparency. Be honest and candid with yourself about what is troubling you and isolate the location. I discovered that my weight issue stemmed from a bigger issue. Identifying the source will explain the symptoms and make for an easier recovery. A leak that shows up on the left side of the basement could have begun on the right side of the roof.

R - Repentance. For yourself, and Godly repentance if needed. Cleanse from self-inflicted bondage based on those that we feel have wronged us. Sincere forgiveness does not wait in expectation of an apology from the culprit in order to heal. Forgive yourself and keep going.

A - Application. Done properly, application yields the better result. Challenge yourself to try new things and trust the process. Proper preparation prevents poor performance. If we are committed to following spiritual order and the God that represents it, then there is no such thing as reality.

I - Invest. Bring a thought into fruition. Make sacrifices to invest time, money, or effort into yourself for the development of goals. Put your money where your mind is. Increase your marketability. Clean up your credit to build your credit score.

N - Nutrition. Every value is not about money; however, value in yourself can translate into additional leverage. A friend of mine named Chris Holder says, "People hear with their eyes." If that's true, then eating the proper food and having an exercise regimen to complement the spiritual and emotional adjustments we make is necessary. Have you ever said, "If I knew then what I know now?" In his book, *Tips to Success*, Mr. Holder also encourages one to see what the end of your success looks like in the beginning of your success journey.

Implementing the T.R.A.I.N. method or creating your own acronym gives you an edge to win and the spirit of distraction becomes less inviting, decreasing its power over your life. Don't feel cheated. Time and chance happen to us all and you don't have to settle for what has happened to you. Failure as the world defines it is not in your DNA. Allow your failures to coach you into greatness, and I'm certain the other authors in this book have a wealth of information that you will find applicable as well. Keep on pushing because the only way that your failures can have a success story is if you refuse to quit!

Overcoming Difficult Obstacles

Kenneth Wilson

As a business owner, coach, and community advocate, I have the daily honor of helping people all over the world. Over the span of my career, I have assisted others in overcoming a wide range of problems from personal family situations to major business issues and I have developed a reputation as a problem solver. This passion to help has been brewing inside of me for a long time. As a child, I knew I wanted to help other people that looked like me overcome the same difficulties I went through. As you may already know, life for black men can be extremely difficult and overwhelming. We often find ourselves lacking in resources, guidance, and support. For us, it feels like we are starting the game of life with negative points. I was exposed to this reality at a very young age through difficult family situations and neighborhood surroundings including drug abuse, extreme violence, and poor conditions. I watched a lot of my friends struggle and even fail to overcome the difficult social and environmental obstacles placed before them.

As I was able to overcome those obstacles, I learned from my situations. Experiences that I previously saw as negative have now become positive because of how I learned from them. I have taken something away from every difficult obstacle I have had to overcome. Here are some tips for how to handle and overcome difficult obstacles in your own life:

Focus on the Solutions and What You Can Control

As a young man, I would often stress out about difficult situations. I would get so nervous and worked up that I would make myself physically sick at times. I would waste my time worrying and stressing, often about things I had no control over. I had to learn to shift my focus from the difficult situation to the solutions. Doing that instantly changed my entire mood, health, and perspective. I was able to focus on the positive solutions instead of the negative situation. Also focusing on solutions allows you to plan and set goals, which is extremely important to overcoming any difficult situation. As a kid, I would write notes of just about everything I wanted to accomplish in life. As I became a little older, I began to expand on those notes. Not only would I write what I wanted to accomplish, but also what steps I would take to accomplish those goals. I recall that on one of those notes I wrote that I wanted to obtain a degree in psychology, because I knew that going to college and getting an education was a way to get out of the neighborhood. I knew to obtain the degree that I would first have to get good grades in elementary, middle, and high school. I also wrote down that I would have to get a good SAT score and stay out of trouble. I would review those notes every couple of months to check my progress. I also used those notes as motivation when times got difficult. If I felt myself beginning to worry or stress out, I would compare my notes to my progress and realize that I was still on the right track and everything was going well.

Focusing on solutions also meant that I would only focus on things that I could control and let everything else go. When I would make my plans, I would only include steps that only I could physically accomplish. I cannot control the actions of other people or acts of God. I wasn't waiting on things to happen; I was focused on making things happen. If I couldn't do anything about it, I would pray and leave it up to God.

I Could Not Do It Alone

As a young person and even as a young man, I would often feel alone. I would be surrounded by people and still feel lonely. It was strange because I was a very well-liked and popular person. I was always able to make friends wherever I went. If I wasn't with friends, I was with my family or my teammates for whatever sport I was playing at the time. As I grew older, I would have a steady girl-friend. So, with all of those people in my life why would I feel lonely? It was because I was ashamed of my situations, and I didn't want to ask for help. I lived and went to school in a very diverse neigh-borhood. Outside of my little hood, there were middle and upper middle-class families. I went to school with them, and often envied their fami-lies and upbringing. I did not want to be the poor black kid or the charity case. I wouldn't tell my friends about my family life. They didn't know that my father wasn't there. I didn't like telling people where I lived, and I didn't invite too many people over to my place.

Once I became a teenager, I began to meet more people from outside of my neighborhood. They would share about their families and neigh-borhoods, and their stories were like mine. They were not ashamed or shy, and they would ask for help when needed. I admired their realness and courage. It allowed me to be open and share, but most importantly I learned how to ask for help. I realized that I was not this helpless unicorn, but I was a human being with issues just like everyone else. I also understood that I couldn't do everything on my own. Yet, even with that understanding, asking for help was still difficult. I had to learn that help comes in many different shapes and sizes. That also allowed me to trust my family, friends, and the people around me. I had to trust that they could help me. I began to have more conversations with my teachers and coaches, and they began to understand more about me. They would check on me to make sure I was ok. They became my support system and the feelings of loneliness began to fade away.

I have three main rules when I ask for help. The first rule is that I ask for help only after I have exhausted my capabilities. This means that I tried and gave it my all, but I couldn't do it. It may also mean that I researched and could not find the answer I need. The second rule is that I cannot be afraid to ask for help. The physical act of asking for help was very difficult for me. It would become easier when I asked for help knowing that I followed the first rule by exhausting all of my capabilities first. The third rule is that if I ask for help, I must accept the possibility of hearing the word no. People have the right to say no, and I never wanted to guilt someone into changing their mind. I also wouldn't let someone's refusal to help be an excuse for me to give up.

I Was My Own Worst Enemy

When situations become difficult, we often revert to the things that make us comfortable. Some people would call these our vices or creature comforts. As a kid, when things got tough at home, I would just want to escape. I was a huge basketball fan. I would ride my bike to a remote basketball court and play by myself for hours. I would practice all my moves and try new ones. I would pretend to be my favorite NBA player and hit the game-winning shot at the last second. I would have so much fun at the basketball court. Then when I got home, I would immerse myself in either homework or video games while eating as many cheese puffs as I could. Then, I would sleep and repeat the next day.

As a young man, I started getting more attention from the ladies. They liked me and I liked them back. Being captain of the football and basketball teams didn't hurt either. When things got too thick and I couldn't handle it, I would always find some willing, cute girl to hang out with. I wouldn't have to talk about my problems or anything negative. All I had to do was give them compliments and make them feel special.

Playing basketball, video games, and girls didn't help me to overcome my difficult situations. All those things did was allow me to not deal with my situations at that moment. I was running away from my problems. Those things made me feel good, when the source of the problem did not. I was allowing myself to become distracted, and I was procrastinating from dealing with the difficult situations. No one else had done this to me. I had become my own worst enemy by allowing it to happen. I learned how to defeat myself by planning and applying discipline to my lifestyle. Like before when I was younger, my plans would give me things to do and work towards, so I wouldn't have time to escape and be lazy or distracted.

Perseverance and Determination

As an athlete, my coaches would often ask us, "How bad do you want to win?" I always thought of myself as a hard-working kid, so that question would often annoy me. I always wanted to win badly. I hated to lose at anything. My problem was that I didn't always like to practice. I would attend practice every day and participate. I would even appear to work hard, but deep down inside I knew I could do more. I could have hustled harder and completed the drills faster. I probably could have run harder in conditioning drills. The problem was that I didn't. I didn't make myself the best possible player. In fact, I cheated myself from becoming the best player I could be. No telling what could've happened if I had pushed myself just a little more. Maybe my training and conditioning would have allowed me to hit the game-winning basket or make that game-saving stop on the goal line.

The same goes for overcoming difficult obstacles. I must be willing to put in the extra work and go the extra mile, no matter what the obstacle is. What is the point of only giving partial effort and work, to only fall short of your goal? The best plans will not work if you don't have the discipline to see them completed in their entirety. Always be honest and ask yourself if you are doing everything you can to overcome the obstacle. I used to have conversations with myself in the mirror in my bathroom. I would look at myself and say, "Am I doing my best? Is there anything else I can do?" If there was something to do, I would go back and review my plan. Maybe I missed a step, or I needed to ask for help.

Conclusion

I have been able to enjoy a successful career of helping others by first being able to help myself. I learned these tips to overcoming difficult obstacles by applying them to my own life first. I was able to overcome, but not without suffering some psychological and emotional wounds along the way. Those wounds became my reminders of those extremely difficult obstacles. I share this knowledge with you in hopes that you can apply these tips when you need to in your own life. I pray that no one else must endure the difficult situations and obstacles that I did. If you have, please find comfort and purpose in these written words, and I hope they help you as they have helped me.

God Doesn't Call the Qualified, He Qualifies the Called

John Edwards

While considering what I would share in this essay, I reflected on many aspects of my life: my birth in Central America; my upbringing in Brooklyn, New York; my family's love; my education; and, a host of other intimate areas of my life that have shaped me into who I am. When I thought about the reader—who he could be and what he would look like—the immediate images that came to mind were of my three amazing sons: an 18-year-old college freshman and 16-year-old twins. As a father, I thought what beneficial nuggets of information could I share with my sons if they were my readers? How could I use my wealth of experience in a meaningful way to leave a road map of sorts? As a professional in the fields of education, training and development, and not for profit organizations, I realized what would be most useful to a reader are the insights I've gained throughout my career that fueled my growth.

To begin, it's important to know something about me. I am an educated black Latino, heavily influenced by black American and Caribbean culture (chalk it up to the Brooklyn experience). I have worked in the corporate and nonprofit sectors, served on several boards, chaired committees, led departments, and managed large-scale initiatives. I have a bachelor's in computer science, and I completed my postgraduate studies in public administration and public affairs. I am 6'3", athletically built with a smooth bald head, and I have a great sense of personal style. This is, by no means, an attempt to humblebrag; within context, these attributes have influenced others' perceptions of me as well as my own self-awareness. My development began with self-awareness.

I spent a lot of time understanding who I am by taking a personal inventory of the multifaceted aspects of my being. I contemplated everything from my physical appearance and the color of my skin to abstract attributes, such as intellect, authenticity, mannerisms, values, and charisma (also known as "swag"). My self-awareness increased as I grew to know myself and understood that how others saw me was equally important, though their perceptions did not always reconcile and were often biased. I was determined to emphasize my strengths and find ways to counter unfavorable perceptions. Being a 6'3" black man from Brooklyn did not always inspire positive images or foster optimistic thoughts for onlookers, but my self-awareness allowed me to preemptively counter perceptions and avoid certain pitfalls or landmines. For example, I knew that if I wanted a career in business, I would have to remove my gold tooth. Although having a gold tooth was a status symbol in my Afro-Latino culture, it would have been a distraction at work. Such distractions are looked upon as: "Somebody never told him something." I have been guilty of such thoughts myself. I recall seeing a young man on the train wearing a business suit with white athletic socks and the suit label prominently showing on the sleeve. I remember thinking, "Where's his dad? A father who was attuned to social norms would have corrected those errors." I remember walking over to the young man and asking him if he was going to an interview. He responded, "Yes." I told him he looked ready, but I suggest that in the future he wear socks that were more conservative (perhaps matching his shoes) and that he remove the name tag on the sleeve. He thanked me for my advice, and I wished him luck.

Understanding where I was in my development as a professional and where I wanted to go, I knew I had to work on improving my communication skills which included how clearly I shared my thoughts and ideas, how concisely I wrote, and how well I paid attention. Self-awareness taught me how to listen critically and how to speak confidently, distinctly, intelligibly, thoughtfully, and purposefully. Once I developed a high level of self-awareness, I began to understand others and their development and influence (or lack thereof), and I gained another essential skill: people-reading.

As a passionate individual, I had to learn how to deliver my passion in an understandable and palatable way. I needed to ensure that my passion wasn't being misconstrued as ABMS—Angry Black Man Syndrome, which wasn't always easy. My ability to put words together sharply, distinctly, and matter-of-factly often got in the way of learning to listen in order to hear. I needed to be open to other perspectives, find value in someone else's opinion, and respectfully respond even when I disagreed. I found power in being able to tailor my passion and counter unfavorable perceptions (consciously or subconsciously). I also realized everyone was not deserving of my strong emotions.

Confidence, too, is extremely important. To gain confidence, I first had to believe that I was good enough and that I belonged. I acknowledged all of my achievements, great and small, even when an accomplishment was simply survival. I harnessed skills into confident energy, not arrogance, which is often misinterpreted. I understood that others' misinterpretations of me had more to do with them than myself and reprogrammed my thoughts of inferiority. My regal history and sound upbringing allowed me to look beyond slavery to develop a greater appreciation of where I had come from. I am a proud, complex black man with many layers, all of which I embrace. I believed in myself, trusted my abilities, and feared less about my path. As I unapologetically took ownership of my life, I learned to praise others, which ensured that those around me felt good in my presence and also felt empowered to be themselves. I positioned myself for greater while I positioned others for the journey as well.

Positioning is another skillset I have learned to develop. This isn't something taught in school; however, with the right amount of awareness, it can be cultivated. Knowing how and when to show up is important. I think about positioning constantly. I think about it in different ways, for instance: How you communicate your accomplishments is part of positioning. Where you sit in meetings is part of positioning. Who you connect to is part of positioning. Positioning has something to do with your personal strategy for representing yourself whenever possible without being an attention grabber but allowing people to know you are present. It might be participating on a panel or a committee or discussing how, through your efforts, you were able to further an agenda or impact the companies' bottom line. Positioning is not only showing up but knowing how to show up. Understanding protocol is a key part of positioning. How you present at a board meeting might look very different from how you present at a brainstorming meeting. Like a game of chess, know your audience and know how they are positioning themselves. Deliver the goods, measure the goods, and communicate your success and impact.

Development, professional or personal, is a lifelong journey not a destination. I have learned that the skills you've used to survive to this point may not be the skills you use on the path forward. Be agile and realize that you're more adaptive than you think you are.

Understanding your values will help guide your journey. I say pay attention to that inner voice. You will find he is quite brilliant. You will never be successful by compromising your values. Now I know you are probably saying to yourself, "There are a bunch of compromised successful people." I say to you, define success for yourself. Is it simply the big home and multiple cars? Is it fame? Or, is it being able to know within yourself that you live by your true values and you are a good person—even the parts and thoughts that no one may ever see?

Accept failures and know that they are a part of the ingredients to your success. Missteps, gaffes, bad decisions, jail time, and addictions are all important to your development and the great design of life. Instead of allowing those failures to victimize you, use them to empower you as a source of strength. You've survived them all. While we wish we may have done some things differently, live with few regrets and embrace who you are today.

Respect is a high value and priority for me. I expect it and I give it. I don't live in a bubble and I know there are many people you will not like or who are not your favorite. However, lean into those relationships and interactions with respect— for yourself first then for others.

Mentorship is a word that is often used but rarely defined, at least the execution of mentorship. Find someone who is willing to pour into you. Find someone who sees value in who you are today and who you can be tomorrow. This person isn't always a parent, family member, or friend. Sometimes it can be someone outside of your expected inner circle. Awareness will be your guide. Oh, that inner voice will come in handy as well when identifying someone who simply criticizes you versus someone who is sharing their perception of you as a mirror would. They may see things in you that you have failed to see for yourself. Finding a mentor(s) is a critical part of the journey. You may have mentors for different stages of your development, and they may not always be the same gender or race. Do not be afraid to ask someone if they would consider being your mentor. For me, that is one of the greatest honors. Stay open!

I want to let you in on my secret weapon and that's the power of levity. The power to know when and when not to use humor. Know that humor can be a way to level the playing field, reduce anxiety, and show your earthly human side as well as project a sense of assurance and confidence.

My last piece of insight is a simple one, sophistication. Carry yourself with dignity and pride. Define that for yourself, and when you achieve it you will know. Being rough around the edges is a great start but the reward is in the transformation.

As men, we have a natural appeal, a way we present ourselves or capture someone's attention. Use your masculine charm, not to deceive but to convince. Please remember that you belong.

Stay blessed.

The Beating Heart of Our Work
Is Service to Others

Gregory Denizard

My parents came to this country at the early age of sixteen from a third world country, Haiti, looking for a better way and an opportunity to succeed. They came with nothing and trusted by faith that through service to others they could contribute to society. They were driven to succeed and never let anything stop them from their dreams. As retired banking and insurance professionals, I reflect on how they instilled those important principles and values into their four children from the early stages of adolescence throughout our adult lives. My parents were true role models of serving others. I too see the importance of have vision and a plan to help others. I am a product of the American dream. I learned that to be successful, you must do well in school, go to college, develop a career, and be a tax paying citizen. I had to learn quickly, as a young man, that the journey was not going to be easy. I learned that many individuals will be responsible for educating me, guiding me, and correcting me on life and success and I will learn best through service.

Dealing with racism and overcoming rejections were my daily challenges throughout my young adult years. Often, I felt like quitting but was driven by the emotional income I received by helping people and serving my community. I was very competitive and used my academic focus to advance my learning through service. I learned to create a voice in various communities that were not receptive to the advancement of a black man. We all want to rise high, overcome our obstacles, and accomplish our dreams in life. One of the things I learned is that as long as we are only focused on ourselves, we will get stuck. Once I took a break from me and was good to someone else, I had more joy in my life and felt more fulfilled in my goals and dreams. God brings people and opportunities in our path so that we can be a blessing. I found out that when I took time to serve and do something good for someone else, I always had increases in my life. I have numerous experiences that may appear to be small and insignificant but helped transformed someone's life. Examples can include visiting a friend who is sick at home; going the extra mile and serving your family; getting up early and helping a friend or neighbor; and volunteering at your job, church, or school.

I want to share a few key lessons I learned by serving others:

1) Learning about serving starts at an early age.

At thirteen years old, my father introduced me to the world of work by helping me get a job as a newspaper carrier with *Newsday* in Long Island. I saw that as an opportunity to serve my community and make a few dollars. I was not prepared for the numerous life lessons I would learn. I soon learned that the person with the route before me was fired for doing a poor job. My experience included daily reminders of adult's dissatisfaction and displeasure with their services prior to me joining. I had to quickly adapt to changing their perception through my service. I learned the importance of being on time, greeting people with kindness, and being a very good listener. I understood early on that people wanted something very specific, personal, and consistent.

As a parent, I understand the importance of my children volunteering and providing services to others. My children have been longtime volunteers, helping with events for children with cancer at annual Thanksgiving dinners. Their compassion for helping others and taking action has been increased by experiencing the impact they can have on others. My daughter, Kayla, learned quickly how fortunate she was and developed a hunger to help children globally in her church, her community, and her school. Children learn to interact with other students and adults in a volunteer setting. They learn to identify what they are good at and develop life skills they can use for the future. In particular, it is amazing exposure for students who may not be sure what they want to do in life but are willing to help. Community service and volunteer opportunities in your school and community are excellent places to expose youth to serving and helping others. I found it important to create family traditions and annual events around volunteering that connect students to their passion.

2) Helping people includes building communities.

In my freshman year at Cornell University, I was recruited to be a big brother for Big Brothers Big Sisters of America. I was paired up with a five-year-old young man from the local Ithaca community. I was reminded by my leaders of my commitment to be a light in this young kid's life. I learned the importance of being a positive role model and helping to shape this child's view of life. Over those four years, I soon realized that service provides an opportunity for others to see their worth through your eyes. In every meeting, interaction, and conversation, I was sharing my dreams and vision and someone else was believing with me. My mentor reminded me often that people forget what you say but never forget how you make them feel. I was filled by the emotional income. Changing one individual at a time was very powerful. That inspired me to enter the youth development profession.

My little brother invited me to many events his parents were hosting in town. As a result, I learned more about the community I was going to school in, and I was able to make a different connection to opportunities that existed right in my backyard. My undergraduate experience in business motivated me to move from the individual impact of service to serving youth in schools, health centers, churches, and communities. I believed that by leveraging the partners in a community, we could reach a larger number of youth through service. The emotional income people get from feeling loved and supported is a major drive to their success. That individual interaction with a child, led me to a successful career in youth development through which I impact students in schools in poor neighborhoods all over the country. I recognized that I received blessings by standing on someone's shoulder and it was my turn to keep the tradition going and transform our communities.

3) Building the faith of individuals transforms people's vision of possibilities.

Our churches and civic organizations are a great place to help people from all walks of life. Churches in particular provide a diverse opportunity for children, youth, and adults to become active in their neighborhood and broader community and provide a service to people. Members of the church gather several times a week and often share a common goal of helping and serving people in the community. Ministry work also encourages us all to spread the good word of love, community, and family. The church provides a family for individuals who may be new to the community, allowing them to connect on a common cause. Serving others gives them an opportunity to develop long-lasting relationships.

As a head usher in my church, I learned that I am responsible for setting the tone of the service for the day by how well people are greeted at the front door. A simple hello and a smile go a long way, making a new person feel welcomed and at home. When you give, God knows how to thank you. He knows how to open the windows of Heaven. My life's journey has been a true blessing, mostly because God has given me an opportunity to serve people in places I would never experience on my own. My church family allows me to do something good for others. People come from different places in their Christian walk and some people come with challenges in their life. I am reminded daily that God created us in His image. He also created us with gifts and talents. Our challenge is to find the gifts. God also showed us how to serve people with very little.

4) Empowering leaders and building wealth is key for growth.

Through my community building journey, I learned that there are five E's for changing someone's life. First is your environment. Your environment influences you. You can be a beacon to someone and provide light in their darkness. Second is your expectations. We believe in good things while we are helping people. Our job as leaders is to find the gifts and talents in everyone we touch. We also believe that good things are possible for all. The third key point to success is execution. In our plan to develop opportunities, we must be laser focused on the efforts of building leaders in our community. The fourth step is experience. We learn through helping people succeed. Lastly, it is very important to be an example for others. Leaders lead from the front and take people along with them.

Wealth building requires you to have a long-term source of income that allows you to have some money left over after you have covered your necessities. Once you have income that's enough to cover your basic needs, you need to develop a proactive savings plan. Once you've set aside your monthly savings goal amount, you need to invest it prudently. These business concepts are simple, but many individuals fail to plan for their life. Empowering our youth and community with financial education is a critical step in building leaders, businesses, and communities. As most are aware, the Bible has a wealth of information and advice about handling money and the ability to build wealth. The book of Proverbs alone provides enough guidance to fill many personal finance books. We must stand in agreement that our career is a valuable asset and serving others will get us further!

"Take a lesson from the ants, you lazybones. Learn from their ways and become wise! Though they have no prince or governor or ruler to make them work, they labor hard all summer, gathering food for the winter."
—*Proverbs 6:6-8 (NLT)*

The Darkness

Maurice L. Williams

As a result of being a fatherless black boy growing up in the ghetto with my mother and little sister, I became a resentful street punk with violent tendencies. I was always tactful in word and mannerism, so my anger and defiance were concealed until I started getting into trouble. At 12 years old, I was arrested for the first time. As a result of not having proper male guidance, I innately searched to form bonds with the men in my neighborhood. Being naive allowed me to be influenced by a flashy dressing popular guy from my block (in Brownsville, Brooklyn). He coerced me into snatching a white lady's pocketbook in broad daylight on 42nd. Street. I was arrested at the scene of the incident. That was the first of my many encounters with the law, jail, and what I now refer to as modern-day slavery.

During my dark years, I committed several juvenile offenses until eventually being sentenced to a year in youth detention. That stint exacerbated my anger and caused me to become more mischievous. I remember feeling as though the world was against me. I felt like my father did not value me, so I needed to make myself valuable. In an unguided and confused mental state, I started a gang with some of my childhood friends. Many of the young brothers I grew up with either went to prison, lost their lives, or were shot and paralyzed in battles over drug money, women, and other elements of street life. In retrospect, I can wholeheartedly state that going to prison saved my life.

Eventually, as a result of all my deviant behavior, I was sentenced to five years for robbery, narcotics, and firearm possession. At that point in my life, I felt like an 18-year-old loser who had failed himself and his loved ones. The consequences of my actions landed me in the penitentiary and the only person I had to blame was myself. While incarcerated, I found out my high school sweetheart was pregnant with my child. Being in jail prevented me from seeing my daughter come into the world. I will never forgive myself for that. As a youngster, I didn't think about the ramifications of my actions. Leaving my pregnant girlfriend in the world to take care of our child by herself was a big mistake. Needless to say, she moved on; the kicker is the fact that she started a family with one of my so-called friends.

Fortunately, prison is where I found out who I truly was. I spent a lot of time soul-searching and discovered some things about myself that I didn't like. I immediately started to hold myself accountable for all the years of ill-advised behavior. I began searching for tools to help me restructure the way I thought. I gained knowledge of myself as a black man by way of Clarence 13X, a student of the Honorable Elijah Muhammed. Clarence 13X is the founder and father of the Five-Percent Nation of Gods and Earths. I was given lessons on degrees of information by one of the older Gods in the jail. I was also given information about Malcolm X (also a student of The Honorable Elijah Muhammed) as well as other influential black men. The information I acquired gave me a deep desire to learn everything I could about the black diaspora. My studies took me beyond the civil rights era, and what I discovered changed the trajectory of my life. I found that the plight of the black man in America is far more significant than money, hoes, and clothes. I learned that our bloodline is connected to kings, queens, scientists, engineers, philosophers, warriors, and other great people. When it registered in my spirit that I am of a great and mighty people, black pride became the foundation of my existence. I vowed to myself that I would never again sell drugs or turn a weapon on my brother or sister. I learned to love myself and people, not just my people but all people.

Although I had a new perspective on myself and life, I did not hit the ground running when I was released. My transition was challenging, and I often thought about reverting to what I was accustomed to. Due to lack of resources, I had to go back to the same environment that glorified the behaviors I was locked up for. However, I knew that I would never again participate in any serious criminal activity. I had friends that I loved who did their thing in the streets and hanging around them became a hindrance. I got arrested a few more times for petty things like smoking weed in public and driving with a suspended license. I eventually grew weary of the hood and the things that go on there. I started to examine what the hood really is and came to the conclusion that the hood is not a place it's a mentality. I discovered that the hood mentality is what I had to get rid of in order to get to the next level. At that time, God had not revealed what the next level was, but I knew my purpose was greater than my present circumstances.

Slowly I trained myself to unlearn some of the bad habits that the ghetto fosters. My goal was not to seek perfection or appear better than another but only to become the best possible version of myself. It was difficult letting go of some of the people and behaviors I was used to. It took a lot of self-assessing to acknowledge the trauma I suppressed in order to survive. Growing up in underprivileged and underserved communities is kind of like living in a war zone. Physical, mental, and spiritual warfare are not always recognized but they are always present in the hood. I didn't realize how deeply rooted my ignorance was until I got my first job. I was hired to do maintenance work in a mental institution where I was required to be professional. I was totally unprepared. Conducting myself professionally was unnatural and scary because I had never frequented a setting that required me to heed directives and dress appropriately while consistently being polite to consumers and co-workers.

The Transition

On my thirtieth birthday, I decided it was now or never. I knew I needed to do some things differently if I wanted to prosper and have longevity. I came to the conclusion that in order to get the results I envisioned for myself, I had to change my surroundings. In a last-ditch effort to overcome the limitations that kept me arrested in my development, I moved to Manhattan. Soon after, I enrolled in an undergraduate college in the heart of Harlem. It was the best decision I ever made. Going to college was a dream I never thought would actually come to fruition; so, when the opportunity presented itself, I took full advantage. I was excited to be the only man on my mother's side of the family to go to college. And for the first time in my life, I was proud of myself. I developed a new kind of self-respect and it felt good. More importantly, I noticed how my mom and family started to appreciate my transition. I recognized that my mom worried about me less and smiled more.

While incarcerated, I had obtained a GED and volunteered as a teacher's aide. Unbeknownst to me, that would be the beginning of my teaching career. As a result of reading *The Autobiography of Malcolm X*, the dictionary and the thesaurus became my best friends. I studied grammar, punctuation, and the different parts of speech which made transitioning into college easier when I came home. My experience as a freshman revealed the disproportionate rate at which black men and women seek higher education. Most of my classes exceeded 20 students, of which I was usually the only black man in attendance. During my sophomore year, I was bestowed the honor of becoming a writing tutor. I aided hundreds of students with successfully completing coursework and research papers. As a result of my success as a tutor, I was inspired to pursue becoming an adjunct lecturer. After earning a bachelor's degree in liberal arts, I went on to acquire a master of science in communication. I was fortunate to have some great mentors who guided me in my quest to become an educator. In hindsight, I can see how I was being groomed to educate. I started as a professional tutor. After graduating, I instructed two independent study courses, ultimately reaching the goal of adjunct professor.

Simultaneously, as I was growing and developing my daughter was too. It is my belief that during her teenage years we were unable to bond naturally because I wasn't there when she was born. It's hard to cope with the fact that the mistakes I made as a young man had a negative impact on our relationship. I now know that a father's love is one of the most important aspects of a little girl's life. Stemming from the estranged relationships with my father and my daughter, I created this acronym for father:

F amily first

A lways present

T hink before speaking or reacting

H ealer

E arner

R ighteousness

The Light

Teaching led me closer to God and allowed me to tap into my purpose. When my spiritual birth occurred, my calling was revealed. The students I worked with were mostly like myself—adults returning to college after years of being out of work or school. This population is unique because of the level of life experience they bring to the classroom. In many courses, several of the participants were older than me and presented a lot of unexpected surprises. Many of them expressed that because I was younger than them I couldn't tell them anything that they didn't already know. I loved those instances because they gave me the opportunity to prove to the rest of the class that I was qualified. Those situations tested my ability to teach through adversity. I developed a style of instructing that meshed communication with compassion in order to effectively deliver lesson plans. I gained trust one student at a time until eventually becoming highly regarded by students and faculty.

As an adjunct lecturer, I instructed communication courses including public speaking, oral communication, news writing, relationship building, and advanced topics in media studies. I was also responsible for developing the curriculum for each course, a skill that helped me with structuring A Father's Love. A Father's Love is the youth development program I founded to help young people recognize the power within and reach their fullest potential. Currently AFL holds workshops in three juvenile detention facilities in New York City, including the infamous Rikers Island. Our services include everything from manhood training to post-release support.

In conclusion, I believe that God is the knower of all things and my obedience to Him has given me tremendous favor. Faith, hard work, and dedication have afforded me the opportunity to live an amazing life. I am blessed to be in a position to use my experience as an example to help my brothers and sisters overcome; I do so eagerly. My testament is that our struggle will never end; therefore, we must keep moving forward while forgiving ourselves for mistakes born of pain, strife, and ignorance. Moreover, recognizing self-defeating thoughts and behaviors is a crucial aspect of personal development. Mastering self-motivation techniques is also integral when it comes to procuring success after achieving goals. Remember that mental health is key, and it is okay to talk to someone when life has become overwhelming.

Health and Wellness:
The Keys to Your Success

Milton Kelly

"... do you not know that your body is a temple of the Holy Spirit within you, whom you have from God? You are not your own..."
—1 Corinthians 6:19 ESV

Did you know that health and wellness are a part of your success? Health and wellness are very important for us to live a successful life. Health puts the focus on the physical and mental body being free from illness, injury, or disease. When we were living our childhood, we were taught about healthy eating. At a young age, we were empowered to stay healthy by eating the right foods and exercising on a daily basis. Wellness is an active process of becoming aware of and making choices toward a healthy, fulfilling life.

Wellness is more than being free from illness, it is a dynamic process of change and growth. It is a state of complete physical, mental, and social well-being not merely the absence of disease or infirmity. Blending health and wellness is a spirited process of change and growth that lasts for a lifetime.

Now, let me share my personal story with you about my journey of health and wellness. In the summer of 2014, I suffered from depression and I was facing being homeless. At that point, I just wanted to give up and take my own life. Before my depression, I was living my best life with joy and happiness. I was fully employed at a financial services company for almost two decades. I had my own apartment and I had a nice amount of savings. I enjoyed spending time with my friends. I loved to travel to different locations every summer. Everything was going great until I lost my job in late 2007. I was being laid off because my whole department was being outsourced. I was able to receive my severance package that lasted for one year. I started to look for another job and went on several interviews. The interviews went well but I didn't get calls. I kept on applying for work. I also applied for different jobs at temporary job agencies. I wasn't successful in obtained those jobs either. I even tried to work with a financial services company that was looking for independent representatives to sell life insurance and recruit individuals to work for them. I gave it a try for about three years, but it wasn't for me. I was living in Jersey City, New Jersey, at that time. I thought that new opportunity was going to be great for me, but I was wrong. I was able to set up meetings with potentials clients, but I just couldn't close the deals. By that time, I went through my savings and eventually I lost my apartment. I was evicted for not being able to pay my rent. I was facing home-lessness and people who I thought were my friends really weren't. I was so disappointed and hurt that I didn't want to live any longer. Finally, I just want-ed to take my own life. One day, I saw a police officer and told him to call an ambulance for me because I was ready to kill myself. They took me to the hospital, and I ended up in the psychiatric emergency room.

The next day, I was discharged and living on the street. I wasn't feeling well, so I ended up in the hospital ER. I stayed there for a couple of days and I was released again. It was a humid summer night and I was living back on the street. This time I felt so much worse that I had a panic attack. I was still depressed, so I took myself back to the hospital. When I arrived at the psychiatric emergency room, the staff gave me a hard time. They asked, "Why are you back? We just discharged you on Friday and now you're back?" I told them I came back because I wasn't feeling any better. They saw me with a bag then asked me, "Where are you coming from? Are you homeless?" I told them that didn't matter; I was there for medical treatment. They checked my blood pressure and it was high. I didn't even know I was walking around with high blood pressure. I am so glad that I advocated for myself; otherwise, I wouldn't be alive today. I stayed in the hospital for about two months. The whole time I was there, I prayed, I read the book of Psalms every day, and I spoke life by using the law of attraction. I was called lazy and stupid by some of the nurses, but I didn't allow their negativity to get to me.

After being discharged from the hospital, I started on my journey of recovery. I learned that one of my mental illness diagnoses, anxiety, is related to hypertension. Anxiety or panic attacks are a part of stress. I take medication for my mental illness but also for my hypertension. I also started to attend an outpatient program for my recovery. I learned so many coping skills and numerous individuals told me that I would make a great advocate for mental illness. I decided that I wanted to become a peer specialist. I didn't do the training right away because my focus was on recovery. I did learn a lot about mental illness. I started to go to mental health and wellness conferences, and I took a trip to Albany, New York, to advocate for mental health programs and affordable housing. I continue to read inspirational and motivational books about mental health and share my story; many individuals are touched by it. If I can just reach one person, I know that I made a difference.

In the summer of 2017, my life changed in a big way. I finally got accepted into the Howie T. Harp Peer Specialist Training Program with Community Access. It was a six-month class training then a six-month paid internship. I learned a lot about the importance of peer advocacy. I didn't know anything about mental health peer specialists until I was in the hospital. I did my six-month internship at Metropolitan Hospital, NYCHHC, and I made a big difference with the patients in the mental health inpatient unit. I was able to show them by example that this is how recovery looks.

Today, I am a mental health peer counselor at Metropolitan Hospital. I am a published author of three books. I am a part of the NYC Suicide Prevention Council. I graduated from Howie T. Harp Peer Specialist Training Program with Community Access. If it wasn't for the grace of God, I wouldn't have made it this far. God is qualifying you for the thing that He has prepared for your destiny. Don't you ever give up. It is time for us to change our conversations. For example, change "I am bipolar" to "I have bipolar disorder." You aren't your diagnosis. Your diagnosis doesn't define who you are. I may have a mental illness, but it doesn't define who I am. Through God, I can do anything I have the desire to do. I am a believer that God is good and faithful. He will never leave me. It was my faith that got me through during my difficult times. I don't look like what I have been through.

What are you going to do about your own health and wellness? Here are the keys to your success through health and wellness:

Health and Wellness - It is very important that you take care of your health and wellness. We must take care of our temple and our mind. Visit your medical doctor for your annual physical exam. Also, if you have problems with your mental health, there is nothing wrong with seeing a psychiatrist and a therapist for help. I make sure that I get my physical exams twice a year. And now that I work in the hospital, I must take my physical exam every year on my job with their doctor and that is great. Also, I see my psychiatrist and my therapist every other month. I also take all of my prescribed medications.

People, Places, and Things - Be careful of certain people, places, and things. You must stay away from people, places, and things that aren't doing you any good. You are the captain of your own destiny. Don't let anyone interrupt your path to success. There are dream killers that don't want you to succeed.

Recovery - Please work on your recovery. Recovery isn't easy, it is a journey and a process. Recovery doesn't happen overnight. It is very important that you follow up on all of your medical, mental health, and substance abuse appointments. Part of your recovery is staying away from individuals who don't want to work on their own recovery. Don't let anyone stop you from recovering.

Self-care - Make sure that you take care of yourself. If you are feeling worn down, make sure you take a self-care day. Self-care is very important. When I am feeling overwhelmed, I call my boss and let her know that I need to take a mental health day.

Self-Improvement - It is always good to improve yourself by learning something new. Part of growth is learning. You are never too old to learn something new. Never stop learning. I am always learning new things on my job at the hospital through trainings and seminars.

Change - Part of being able to experience success is being able to change. We must be willing to change. If we aren't willing to change then we won't experience growth. Change starts from within.

Reading - You should always be willing to read books. I love to read motivational, inspirational, and Christian books. We all need to be empowered. We need to feed our mind with positive messages. We should clean our mind on a daily basis.

Change your vocabulary - The tongue is powerful. Be sure to taste your words before you spit them out. James 3:5 (TLB) says, "The tongue is a small thing, but what enormous damage it can do." You must change your negative words into positive words. Impossible = I am possible. I can't = Yes, I can. Also change your negative conversation into a positive one. Remember life and death are in the power of the tongue. Choose your words wisely.

Give back - The main reason I am a mental health peer counselor today is because I wanted to give back what was given to me. When you give back to your community, you are actually making the community much better and that is a true success.

Support - Make sure you are getting support from your family, friends, and peers. Support goes both ways, so make sure you give them your support as well.

Spirituality - Whatever your belief system is, let that empower you. I am a Christian, I believe in God, I go to church, and I read my Bible and pray. Prayer and faith are the foundations of my success and recovery. Prayer and faith without works are dead. You must put your prayer and faith into action.

Take responsibility - Stop blaming others for the mess that you created. Before you blame others for your mistakes, take a look in the mirror. Placing the blame on other individuals will leave you powerless to change your experience. Taking responsibility for your beliefs and judgments gives you the strength to change the experiences in your life. When I was going through being homeless and dealing with my illness, I never blamed others. I took responsibility for my own actions.

Self-investments - The best thing I ever did for myself was to make investments into myself. The greatest thing you can do is to free yourself from the baggage that is holding you back or the things you can't control. Invest your time and energy into the things you can control, like your attitude.

During my recovery, I invested my time and energy into changing my attitude about life. It is amazing that God created my life and I am so grateful.

Validation - Don't wait for someone to validate you. Be your own cheerleader. After I was released from the hospital in 2014, I worked on my recovery and I learned to begin to relinquish my ego. Now, I don't feel compelled to prove to anyone how busy I am in an attempt to validate someone else's sense of worth. I know my own worth.

Treat yourself - I now take myself on a date by going out to a nice restaurant, going to the movies, and even buying myself new clothes and other things I desire. Recently, I purchased an Amazon Fire tablet and I am enjoying my new toy. I feel really good and proud of myself. This is part of my therapeutic time.

In conclusion, without taking care of our health and wellness, our temple (body) and mind will not function well. Our temple and mind will lack the energy and enthusiasm needed to do the things we enjoy the most. I am a success if I get up early in the morning and get plenty of rest at night. In between, I will do whatever I want to do. That's what success means to me. The message I want to leave with you about success is that whatever dreams you've got your eyes set on, please make sure that you use the power of self-care and take care of your health and wellness if you really want to conquer your goals. I am a living witness. I am not just talking about it, I practice what I preach. Whatever mistakes you have made, please forgive yourself and move forward in your journey of success. Great health and wellness are the best wealth and success.

A Gift to Persist: The Art of Moving Forward

Von Franklin

I want to start this chapter with a quote from Zig Ziglar—"You don't have to be great to start, but you have to start to be great."

Your trials in life can either push you up or your view of those trials can pull you down. As a child my views of life were and still are pretty different. I am the fourth oldest child of eight siblings from a single parent household with my earliest memories beginning in Harlem.

I started school at the age of eight which was considered late. Again, I am the fourth child of eight—seven boys and one girl—so I was a pretty rough kid. In my young years, we lived at 204 West 140th. Street, Apt 9. I went to Public School 123 Mahalia Jackson where I started in a second-grade class. From the very start, I have been playing a game of keep up.

From age eight to eleven years old, I was evaluated at the city college campus in Harlem on 140th Street and Amsterdam. Those evaluations were in place to see if I would be left back or pushed forward to the next grade. I learned very early that I had an extraordinary memory and I used my memory to benefit me in class. I would sit and memorize the multiplication table chart, names, and certain techniques. I really enjoyed school as a kid.

In the summer of 1989, my mother took us to Far Rockaway, Queens, to spend the summer with our Aunt Berta who was sick at the time. Aunt Berta was definitely a second mother to me so that summer was pretty memorable.

That summer was also the beginning of an awakening for me in the way I saw myself.

We returned home at the end of August to find our apartment door wide open and the apartment cleaned out.

My mom screamed a horrible scream and nearly fainted. She went to speak to the super who said he knew nothing about it.

For the next two years, my mother, my seven siblings, and I spent time in the New York City shelter system. We ended up in an awesome (see there's that "different" thinking) shelter in Harlem on 129$^{th.}$ Street and Convent Avenue. I started the fourth grade at Public School 129. My teacher's name was Mr. Hinton. I don't know if it was the fact that he was a male teacher or the fact that he was black, but Mr. Hinton was definitely one of my favorite teachers. I learned a great lesson from him. "Always be aware of how you treat people especially when you don't know how they see you."

By the end of 1990 or early 1991, we moved to the Bronx. We lived at 2729 Davidson Avenue. I remember starting the fifth grade as a transfer student. I can recall not knowing what I wanted to be. That was the first time the question "What do you want to be?" meant something to me.

I was always a talented kid. I was always singing and doing voice impersonations and sound effects. I figured it out, I wanted to be an actor. I think if I would have had a little more positive reinforcement, I would have pursued that dream wholeheartedly. I didn't know at the time that I was living through someone else's eyes and fears.

That happens quite often to young people. We live our lives through the fears and failures of our parents and other respected adults. By the time I was twelve, I lived with my aunt in Queens full-time. I was traveling back and forth to the Bronx to go to school. Living with my aunt was difficult at first but rewarding to this day. My aunt, a 52-year-old single mother of two, was a rape survivor, a recovering alcoholic, and the first person at her age that I had ever witnessed pursuing a high school diploma. I never knew how much that affected me until we ended up in the shelter again. I started to see my life in a different way, through fearful eyes.

I was concerned about my future. And at the rate things were going, I felt like I needed to do something to change the course that life had seemingly decided for me.

I was 16 years old then. Sixth grade was long gone. I was skipped to the ninth grade and school seemed like a joke. I remember getting into a fight on my first day of ninth grade over the fact that I understood the work and for being called a nerd. By the tenth grade, school had become a very stressful part of my young life. In January 1997, I ran away from home and ended up a ward of the state. By that time, I was on a mission to gain a better educational opportunity or find another option.

In my pursuit to improve myself, I was selected as an early youth council member with ACS. That was where I really became aware of my ability to assist people. Fast forward a bit. I completed culinary school in 2001, just a year before I received my GED, and enjoyed a start in a career in food services.

My time as a ward of the state had given me a great desire to serve. I thought that a career in culinary arts would satisfy that desire that had been growing inside of me since my days in foster care. In the foster care agency, in the summer of 2003, we created a program called Teens at Parks. I had become a consultant for the Parks Department of New York City after volunteering from 2001-2003 to teach my own cooking classes. I stayed with the Parks Department until 2005 when I started pursuing bigger and greater challenges. Fast forward a bit and we're close to present day. I was living in Rockaway Park during the disaster that was Superstorm Sandy. I lost everything. My landlord had conveniently illegally evicted me, so I couldn't receive FEMA benefits. I found myself in the shelter for the third time in my adult life. Though I was always able to obtain great employment opportunities, housing in New York was a different obstacle.

In early 2012, after a long day of work on January 12, I'd return to a working shelter on 82nd. and Columbus to find that I had no bed and was marked as a curfew violator. That night, I received a call from my sister stating that I could stay with her in the Bronx for a bit. I collected all of my belongings and jumped into a cab to the Bronx. My mom had an apartment in the Mill Brook Houses in the South Bronx. I had stayed there a few years prior as work with the Parks Department was a few blocks away at the St. Mary's Recreation Center. After a few weeks of living with my sister in the Bronx, a program opened in the Mill Brook Houses called Jobs Plus. I began volunteering with the program. Through my volunteering, the tenant association president, Ms. Priscilla Jameson, connected me with a nonprofit organization called Community Voices Heard. I began canvassing the Mill Brook Houses, Patterson Houses, Mitchel Houses, and many more working for NYCHA through Community Voices Heard. I realized that what I was going through as far as losing my apartment and all of my property was being pushed out of my mind as I became more involved in assisting people in various degrees of housing distress. I have taken the focus off of me and put it on others. That created a great sense pleasure and reward for me.

In the summer of 2012, I was given an opportunity to create a community garden space in the Mill Brook Houses. From 6:00 a.m. until about 2:00 p.m., I would water, prune, and plant as needed. The space was reclaimed in 2014 by the New

York City Housing Authority. After the NYCHA reclaimed the garden space on June 4, 2014, with the help of Legal Zoom, Mobile Office Media LLC was created. The idea was and still is to combat negative stereotypes and the lack of positive media coverage in many black and brown communities and show that there are some extraordinary people in these communities also.

I wanted to be able to do more, but then I noticed something about myself. I never allowed myself an opportunity to feel like a victim. I had gone through many situations in my life, but there was always just one way to go... and that was up. With this notion, I want you to create a platform to give light to individuals that don't seem to have it. Uplift those that need it the most, then show those who have never seen it that this seemingly impossible and monumental feet is possible.

In my spare time, I started doing some independent campaigning for individuals by promoting their crowdfunding efforts with small posts and business reposts via social media platforms such as Instagram, Facebook, and Twitter. I began formulating ideas on how to share amazing stories from the black and brown communities of New York through Mobile Office Media, LLC. My intent was to create a space to spotlight entrepreneurs and small businesses in the South Bronx. Mobile Office Media started as an idea through my time as an organizer and an actor. I was increasingly frustrated at the limited number of outlets speaking about people in underprivileged communities doing amazing things. The opportunity to create an outlet to talk about what I had experienced and seen in this incredible inner-city space seemed to be worthwhile. Instead of being angry that there were no media outlets covering good stories coming out of communities like the South Bronx, I decided to create an outlet of my own to speak about the little guy and the hard-working individuals that really aren't spoken of. My mission is to show that communities like this produce some of the world's most amazing gems. The journey has been a long and sometimes rewarding one. I've learned that even when things seem to be at their lowest there's always a bright side. Things could be worse. I'm grateful for the opportunity and the outlet Suited for Success has given me to build my network and followers. This has not been a journey without struggle, yet this has been a journey with persistent moves forward.

A good friend of mine named Ash Cash told me a while ago, "You have every bit of potential that you see in yourself." I want to take this time to thank several wonderful mentors I have had in my life: Mr. Vurnell Martin who gave me my first opportunity to run my first culinary class at the St. Mary's Recreation Center for the New York City Parks Department. My pastor, Michael Christopher Peace, who always told me that I was the bravest guy he knows. I don't know why. And last but not least my aunt, Alberta Franklin, who showed me without saying it that there is no age cap on making tremendous change in your life. If you want it, go get it. The only boundaries are the ones that reside within you.

Always remember these few things:

1) For the young man or young woman reading this, always have a suit. Another mentor of mine would always say to me, "To attract a million dollars at least look like a hundred thousand." That idea always holds its place in my life because wearing a suit always makes me see myself in a better light.

2) Always carry gum or breath mints. You never know who you're going to be talking to. And if you talk a lot like me, you don't want to offend anybody; you don't want people to leave before you make your point.

3) Optimism is key. Things will look tremendously horrible and sound disastrously devastating. A small hint of optimism goes a long way. Be as optimistic as possible. The potential is up to the way you see it. If you don't see potential, you will not get anywhere. Be optimistic.

4) Get some great people around you. I know it sounds easy; we say these things a lot and a lot of mentors say these things, but how can you do that when you don't know great people? Take your time. Get close to people that have the same ideas as you, who motivate you, and who don't let you off the hook. Those are the people you want to be around. They're going to call you, they're going to text you, they're going to find a way to communicate with you. Those are the people you need to be around.

What number we on? Oh, right...

5) Write. Get a notepad, a booklet, or if you have a smartphone use the notepad in your smartphone. The notepad has a little microphone setting. If you press the microphone, you can actually speak into it and it will write down what you're saying. So, going forward, always have your ideas written down. And keep going back to read them. Be aware of what you're putting

down on paper because it will help you and it will tell you what you need to do next.

Thank you for taking the time to read this chapter. I hope that it has blessed you in some way, shape, form, or fashion. Stay blessed. My name is Von Franklin of Mobile Office Media. Peace.

If You Are Not the Lead Dog, the View Never Changes

Jerry Francois

"If you're not the lead dog, the view never changes."
—Dan Pena

This is one of my favorite quotes because I deem it to be true and relevant to my life. My name is Jerry Francois. I was born to parents of Haitian descent on September 24, 1984, at Woodhull Hospital. I grew up in an apartment located in Crown Heights until I was about seven years old. My parents worked tirelessly to provide the best education for me. I attended private school from kindergarten through twelfth grade. My family and I moved to Canarsie in 1990. As proud homeowners, my family was one of the first black families to move to that area of Brooklyn. We had more space. It's pretty fair to say I was raised very well. I grew up playing baseball. I started playing at the age of 11 for the Police Athletic League. I played until high school.

At the age of 16, my life took a turn when I found out my mother was diagnosed with stage 3 stomach cancer. I was devastated. My mother was my rock, my everything. She was the type of mother that would always put me before any of her needs. She would not sleep until I came home, and everything she did was with unconditional love. She unfortunately lost her battle with cancer and in March of 2001 my beautiful heart went home to be with God. I was just 16 years of age when that happened, and I was filled with so much grief and heartache that around the age of 17 I decided a change was needed. I moved to Fort Lauderdale, Florida, for a change of scenery. I lived with my uncle, Delano, who was a pastor and a mentor to me. He instilled many principles into me which I did not take advantage of at the time; however, those principles played a key role 15 years later. Delano's two sons, Godson and Richie, who also lived in the house, were like brothers to me. Delano kept that house well grounded. Despite my new living environment, I still managed to stray off course due to my own foolish and selfish reasons. Suddenly my whole perspective on life changed for the worst. I lost focus of my goals, I dropped out of college, and I started chasing women and hanging out with drug dealers. My mindset was to get money by any means necessary.

In 2006, I decided to move to South Carolina to be a part of an organization that was trafficking cocaine and weed from Atlanta to South Carolina. Every weekend I was in a different hotel, I partied, and I lived like a rock star. I also had plenty of options when it came to the ladies. I didn't do too much talking because my money spoke for itself. Sounds cocky and, yeah, it was. But in 2007, reality set in when I was pulled over on I-75 with two keys of cocaine and $20,000. The drugs and the money were stashed in a hidden compartment. When I was asked to get out of my vehicle, I began to take more notice of the three police vehicles and the K9 dog that eventually found that hidden stash. Was that a coincidence? Of course not. That tip or snitch was the end of that life for me. I was sentenced to five years mandatory minimum at The McKean Camp Federal Correctional Facility. In the federal system, you have to serve 87 percent of the time you've been sentenced to. Prior to sentencing, I was offered a reduced sentence of only two years if I would cooperate by exposing who was running the operation. I refused to cooperate with the police and in turn served three years and ten months out of the five years I was sentenced to. Prison will either make you or break you! For me, it made me a stronger person. I took that time to get my mind, body, and spirit together. Now, I don't want to make it seem like prison was all sweet; it has its ups and downs because you will be tested. I stood strong through the three times I was tested because I was ready to die for my respect.

"Tough times don't last but tough people do."
—Robert Schuller

Respect is very important in prison. We have a saying and it goes like this, "Penitentiary rules in effect." That means respect yourself and everybody around you. In prison, my daily work routine was to get up to go work in the kitchen at 6:00 a.m. I was a dishwasher. I worked the breakfast shift. I was only getting paid $34 a month. That's worse than minimum wage. Actually, it's considered modern-day slavery. The flip side to that is I had access to chicken, fish, and fruits, which are like cash in the prison system. Even though I only worked the breakfast shift, I had all-day access to the kitchen. So, I would strategize a way to wrap the chicken and fish, tuck it in my pants to bring it back to the dorm, sell half, and keep the other half to cook. I used a microwave to cook fried rice with honey, fried noodles, and bake cheesecakes. In my dorm,

I was the one selling fruits in a jar for two tuna packs which is considered $2. I made a decent living, plus I had close friends and family who would send me money as needed and write me letters.

An outside support system will help keep you sane. Six months prior to my release date, I was calling all of my reliable resources so that they could position me with a job. By the grace of God, Christian Cultural Center (one of the biggest churches in Brooklyn) granted me back a position in the logistics department. Jail was the first phase to becoming an entrepreneur. Phase two was CCC, which taught me interpersonal skills, hard work, hands on skills, customer service skills, and much more.

"Self-esteem: The degree to which one has a feeling of worth, value, and significance as a person."
—Dan Pena

I was one of the best employees to ever work in my department. I went with positive energy, passion, and a phenomenal work ethic. I was always on time and the last one to leave. I was willing to work overtime all the time. At one point, I was working seven days a week. I became selfish for my goals. I was also granted another opportunity to work at a charter school called Culture Arts

Academy. I started as a maintenance worker for the first couple of years. I worked hard and showed my worth, so notice was taken. I was then offered the position of facilities manager. I went into the position with great appreciation and motivation.

By taking on that position, I learned so much about leadership. One thing that was natural for me to do was to lead from the front not the back. I made sure everybody worked as a team. That can be a struggle at times. In the words of John Maxwell in *The Law of the Lid*, "Leadership ability determines a person's level of effectiveness." So basically, the law states that how well you lead determines how effective you are. Furthermore, John Maxwell explains that the lower your ability to lead, the lower the lid will be on your potential. While the higher your ability to lead, the higher the lid will be on your potential. Knowing that, I took full responsibility for what was going on under the surface. After numerous meetings and personal development courses everything went smoothly as it would at any organization, right?! WRONG! Any problem solved will be replaced, immediately, by a larger more complicated one. That was where phase three came about in my journey to becoming an entrepreneur. Becoming a manager brought out the natural leader in me. Taking the position without any managerial skill showed that I am a risk taker. Dan Pena once said, "Most successful people do it poorly until they do it well. Just keep blundering along. You can't wait until it's exactly right. The product of your quest for perfection is... paralysis."

Timing and Positioning

In the month of October in 2015, fate led me to my beautiful queen. This beauty was standing in my then workplace, Cultural Arts Academy. We locked eyes briefly and I looked away as to not intimidate her, but I knew in that moment I had to get to know her. I immediately began to think of all of the nonbasic ways to get her attention. When a couple of days went by and I stumbled upon this beauty again at Nordstrom Rack, I knew that it was no coincidence. I immediately positioned myself to bump into her. Then, I began with the pleasantries of introducing myself. In turn, I asked her name. "My name is Stephie," she said. Of course, I brought up the "You look familiar" line, even though I knew exactly where I knew her from. I was eager to ask for her number, but I kept my cool and showed patience as in a game of chess, because every move I made would get me closer to capturing my queen. I knew I would see her at work.

By Monday, I couldn't wait any longer as that patience I exuded was running out. The minute I saw that beautiful face with her beautiful brown eyes, I immediately asked for her number and the exchanges were made.

That day when I got home, I called every woman I was talking to at the time and told them I would no longer be available. I knew that this woman was going to be my wife. We began dating and by the third month we began an exclusive relationship—she was my lady and I was her man. We began our journey together and went on numerous adventures. We have vacationed and explored a few cities as well as countries. We even visited our parents' homeland for the first time. I am truly blessed to have found someone who I can call my friend, someone whom I fall in love with over and over again. On January 19, 2019, she became my fiancée. I found the woman of my dreams. She is truly my better half. Together we are an unstoppable force and I cannot wait until July 9, 2020, when she will officially become my wife.

The Mentor-Mentee Relationship

Mentoring is a partnership between two individuals, the mentor and the mentee. In considering the roles of the mentor, he or she must wear many hats throughout the process. The mentee, the student, needs to absorb the mentor's knowledge and have the ambition and desire to know what to do with that information. As for me, I gained my mentorship through my team, Dream Team Global, which consists of 12 members. When I'm amongst these kings, they hold me accountable for everything I say and do.

We have conference calls Monday through Friday at 10:30 a.m. to discuss what we're grateful for and business. Also, we meet once a month to discuss the status of our investments. You cannot be a high achiever while associating with low performers. It is key that you seek out high-quality relationships to fill your life with. People who will push you, convict you, and challenge you to rise above mediocrity.

Take Action

Phase four of my journey was finally deciding to resign from my full-time job. It was time to take action and start building generational wealth for my family. I would rather work hard for four years straight and take a chance on my own ideas, than work 40 years for someone who wasn't afraid to take a chance on theirs. Before my mother passed away, she laid the foundation for me and my father.

I'm following her blueprint for being financially astute by becoming a real estate investor. I procrastinated for years due to fear, uncertainty, and doubt. I thought that taking action was reading books and watching YouTube videos. To achieve the success that I wanted, I needed the hands-on experience. Feel the fear of failure and take action anyway. No more sitting and waiting to have all of the information and the perfect plan laid out.

The Master Chapter

Hubert Lee Guy Jr.

Life is a set of strategic obstacles. How you maneuver through them determines how you finish. My journey began in Battle Creek, Michigan, 01:18 hours, on Wednesday, October 16, 1974. Born son of Hubert and Alice Guy, youngest sibling of Michael, David, LaMonica, and Regina. Growing up in a modest two-bedroom house in the suburbs, our parents always made sure we had. My father had a good union job with the local paper mill and my mother was one of the top cosmetologists in our city. Our house was where all the kids on the street came to hang out and play all day until my mom made everybody go home. Parents and kids were definitely close-knit in our neighborhood and if you got in trouble at somebody else's house then you were definitely getting in trouble when you got home. I remember having epic games of kickball for hours on the street and family against family hoop games in our backyard. I can say that I truly enjoyed my childhood. But my seven-person household was just a small part of a much bigger and notorious Guy family.

Another part of the family was known for being black revolutionists. They were extremists to say the least. They engaged in police shoot outs, and waged war on other families and whoever or whatever stood in their way. They were always in the news for something. They had red, black, and green houses and when we visited them it was like attending a Black Panther rally. I never quite understood it when I was younger, and I would be ashamed or get teased for being a part of the Guy family. But as I got older and came into my own, I embraced my family name in a few different ways.

My parents had divorced by the time I was 13. My sisters stayed with my dad and my brothers had already left home. My mom and I stayed with my aunt in the projects until she could get us a place of our own. I was a latchkey kid from junior high through high school. My mom worked two jobs, so I spent a lot of my time alone which led to me getting into trouble with the law, fighting, carrying guns, stealing, and lying. I eventually was expelled from high school and had to obtain my GED. My mother would always tell me: "Read your Bible" and "Go to barbering school." Those seven loving words molded me into the man I am today.

After obtaining my GED, I went on to serve in the United States Air Force as a transportation and mobility specialist. After separating from the military under honorable conditions, I attended DeVry University in Atlanta, studied computer information systems, and eventually got into retail and restaurant management. On December 17, 2002, I moved to New York City. On that day, the city of New York had one of its worst blizzards in years and I took that as a sign that my new journey wasn't going to be easy. I was right. It was really tough being in New York with no family, not having anyone to call to say: "I'm coming over for dinner" or "Can I come crash for the night?" I had no one to turn to; everything I dealt with was on my own. Food, shelter, money, life itself was a constant struggle and at times I wondered if it was all worth it. So many times, I felt alone and wanted to give up, but I never did. To compound my struggles and pain, in April of 2004, my mother had a stroke on Easter Sunday. Two days later, my father passed away.

Talk about an emotional overload and whirlwind of feelings. I was struggling in New York and now with my parents. I felt like I couldn't take anymore. I went home to Michigan for a month and almost didn't go back to New York, but I knew I had to return and finish what I started. Upon my return to New York, I received an insurance settlement from my father's passing and paid for my barbering school. On June 4, 2004, I began my barbering career. It was the beginning of my second life journey. My road to becoming a head master barber for TV and a national educator wasn't easy. I couldn't cut my way out of a paper bag when I first started cutting hair. I was absolutely terrible. Here's a funny story behind how I got into my first shop in Harlem. I went to a well-known shop and spoke with the owner. I told him that I had been cutting for years and I was nice with it. So, he got me a few heads to cut and told me to do a light Caesar, skin fade, and taper. I zeeked (messed up) every last one and the shop owner was staring at me with a "What the hell did you just do?" look on his face. He said he would call me, but I kinda felt like he wouldn't. He didn't.

All week long, I thought about how I could get a second chance. The following Monday, I called and disguised my voice to see if he was there again. I asked, "Are you guys open today?" He said, "Yes," and asked if I was looking for a particular barber. I said, "No." I really just wanted to know if he was there so I could redeem myself. When I walked in, he looked at me like, "What are you doing here?" I said, "Last week I had a bad week and I want to get another shot." He agreed to give me that shot, but I had the same result as the first time. I told him barbering was what I wanted to do and how determined I was to be the best and work hard at my craft every day. He saw that I was serious and passionate and gave me a chance. Without that break, I'm not sure how my barbering career would have gone. I worked hard, had patience, stayed focused, and slowly mastered my skills and dreams.

The birth of my first child and namesake, Hubert III, and soon the births of my son, Daniel, and my daughter, Nyimah, really made me buckle down more in my career and in life. Dealing my children's mothers wasn't always the easiest either. In time, with growth and patience, we understood that our kids' lives were much bigger than any issue we had. Words can't describe how much I love being a father. No matter how hard my day was or when I felt I couldn't go on, I would think about my kids and all would be right with the world. Having a strong, loving bond with my children is better than any connection I've ever made in life. My world needs them just as much as they need me. I wasn't living for myself anymore, I had three beautiful little blessings that counted on me. The stakes were higher, so I had no choice but to make things happen. It is very important to me to be an exceptional father and role model for my kids, to show them that you can achieve anything if you assert yourself.

Even as I got better and better over the years at barbering, it just seemed like I wasn't getting anywhere in my career. I saw my peers elevating—doing educational seminars, starting product lines, cutting celebrities, and working on TV shows. All the things I wanted to do. I was never jealous, nor did I have any hate, I just worked even harder to get to where I wanted and needed to be in my career. I have been blessed through hard work, dedication, and perseverance to work with celebrities, athletes, have youth barbering programs, teach thousands of students, and work on national commercials and videos. I was the head master barber for season 3 of the Emmy award–winning Amazon show *The Marvelous Mrs. Maisel* and for *The Code* on CBS. I am also the national barbering educator for the IATSE Local 798 Makeup Artists and Hair Stylists Union in New York. I've done hair for *Orange is the New Black*, *Power*, *The Last O.G.*, *Saturday Night Live*, Men's Wearhouse, Nike, New Era, the New York Knicks' Garden of Dreams Foundation, and the shows "West Side

Story, "Newark, "Tommy," and "Almost Family," and I have done countless pop-up shops. I have also been blessed to be an actor, TV and event host, recording artist, and entrepreneur.

As an actor, you can see me on season six, episode three of the Netflix hit series *Orange is the New Black* playing CO Bay in the opening scene. I've also been on *Seven Seconds*, *Blue Bloods*, *Gypsy*, *Blindspot*, and *Law & Order*. I've also performed in plays for various theater companies. I've had a national internet and radio promotion with Gillette titled, "What Women Want." And I've had the honor and privilege of hosting shows for the SITA (Success in the Arts) Awards, NYC Fashion Live, the Keri's Korner Radio Show, and more. I also produce and host my own public access television show called *The Actors Cut* which airs on MNN in New York every Wednesday at 5:00 p.m. It can be live streamed on mnn.org or viewed on my YouTube channel: Hubert Guy. My show has featured Emily Tarver and Vicci Martinez, Papa Wu, Taryn Manning, PK Kersey, and many other up and coming recording artists, actors, public figures, entrepreneurs, and more. As a recording artist I have always had a love for music. It was 1986 when I started middle school, and hip hop was starting to take over. My love for hip hop grew, and I began writing and performing as a solo artist. My first single, "Love Song," debuted on the local Battle Creek, Michigan, DJ MATRIX radio show in 1990. Over the years, I have performed at several open mic events and have had several radio appearances across the country promoting my music. In 2018, I released the singles "The Most," a club banger (the video is on my YouTube channel Hubert Guy); "Mezmorized," a smooth track for the ladies; and "Heighty Hi," an old school remake of singer Lee Michaels with St. Ends.

I also have goals of opening businesses in my hometown of Battle Creek, Michigan. I plan on giving back and helping to rebuild, rejuvenate, and revitalize my community and town. It's important that when we reach a certain level, we extend a helping hand to those in need. I don't necessarily mean money either. You can provide knowledge, understanding, and insight to someone who can prosper from it and in turn help others as well. My town made me into the man I am today, and I wouldn't want to be from anywhere else. I've always been close with my childhood friends Shanay Settles, Doug Dzwik, and especially my cousin Diallo Dotson who is like a brother to me. I have pretty much known them my entire life. They are my three "day ones" for sure and I would do anything for them.

I look back on the trials and tribulations I've been through and thank God all the time for keeping me alive, safe, and in my right mind. I know that with my faith I can handle anything. You have to recognize your potential to be able to nurture, grow, and capitalize on it in a positive way and that comes from having good morals, values, beliefs, and an attitude to want to overcome any obstacle in your path. My mother and father raised me this way and made sure that I took accountability for my actions so that I would learn from my mistakes and grow from them. Remember that no matter how hard things get, even if you can't see the other side, don't give up. Keep elevating, keep striving, and keep living to be the best you can be every day of your life.

My favorite word is progression. As defined in the dictionary it is the process of developing or moving gradually towards an advanced state. You are a unique individual unlike anyone else, so you are already a standout. When you understand that, you can find your purpose and take it to the next level. I truly do not know where I would be without barbering, it saved my life. It is a skill that you can take with you anywhere in the world and make a living. I enjoy being able to share my knowledge, help to start someone's career, or enhance others' techniques. I am very passionate about life and what

I do, and I thank God for blessing me and using me as this vessel for His will.

If you are interested in becoming a barber, contact your local barbering school. In the Bronx, New York, they have the Bronx EOC which has a free barbering program along with other free programs. You can find more information at bronxeoc.org or you can go to your local barbershop and inquire with the owner or master barber about working underneath them as an apprentice. Every state has different laws so make sure you check with the licensing bureau in your state about rules and regulations.

In closing, I would like to thank my beautiful and wonderful wife, Dierdre Harris, for loving me and my children, being my rock, and always supporting me in everything I do. I love you with all my heart. To my Lord and Savior. Giving all honor and praise to God—my creator, my foundation, my all. Without You I would be lost in this wilderness. Thank you for continually guiding me and giving me strength to continue my life's journey. Thank you for my life. I am forever grateful.

Always remember to stay focused. God bless you.

Sources

Unless otherwise indicated, scripture quotations are from the Holy Bible, King James Version. All rights reserved.

Scriptures marked ESV are taken from English Standard Version®. Copyright © 2001 by Crossway, a publishing ministry of Good News Publishers. All rights reserved.

Scriptures marked NIV are taken from the New International Version®. Copyright © 1973, 1978, 1984, 2011 by Biblica, Inc.™. All rights reserved.

Scriptures marked NLT are taken from the New Living Translation®. Copyright © 1996, 2004, 2007, 2013 by Tyndale House Foundation. All rights reserved.

Scriptures marked TLB are taken from The Living Bible copyright © 1971 by Tyndale House Foundation. Used by permission of Tyndale House Publishers Inc., Carol Stream, Illinois 60188.

About the Authors

PK Kersey has been married for over 25 years to his wife Keenya and has twin boys (Kell and Kye). He was an employee for NYS DMV for over 24 years, where he progressed to office manager over three offices. PK left the DMV to pursue his desire to assist men in obtaining work and to help HS students attend prom and graduation while looking sharp in professional attire. PK co-founded the nonprofit organization That Suits You. Since the inception of the organization, they have assisted over 8,000 individuals in obtaining the clothing, information, and motivation needed to go to the next level in their lives.

PK is also an author. His bestselling book, *Suited for Success, Vol. 1*, includes stories of 25 black men written to inspire the next generation.

Learn more at
www.thatsuitsyou.org

Chip Baker is a teacher and coach that has been in the education profession for 20 years. He is originally from Hearne, Texas, and attended college at West Texas A&M University. At West Texas A&M, he played football and graduated with a bachelor of science in sports and exercise science/special education. He has a master's degree from Sam Houston State University in educational leadership.

Throughout his career, Chip has received the teacher of the year award twice on his campus, he has published several articles, he has been a two-time author, and he has been a head football coach/athletic director. He has a YouTube channel (podcast), *Chip Baker- The Success Chronicles*, where he interviews people from all walks of life to discuss their path to success.

Chip is currently a teacher and coach at Oak Ridge HS in Conroe, Texas. His motto is "Live. Learn. Serve. Inspire. Go get it!"

To connect, email him at
chipbakertsc@gmail.com

Frank E. Brady is an award-winning poet, educator, and youth engagement specialist. He has appeared on BET, Soultrain.com, *The Source Hip Hop Magazine*, and the Huffington Post. His recent accomplishments include being named a digital correspondent for BET's online series, *What's at Stake*, and being named the Black Enterprise's B.E. Modern Man of the Year for 2018. He is a recipient of The National Healthcare Advertising Gold Award for his work on the Community of Caring marketing campaign with the Cornell Scott-Hill Health Center.

Frank holds a bachelor of communications from Southern Connecticut State University. He is the co-founder of Driven2Inspire LLC, where he provides personal and professional development for colleges, corporations, and non-profit organizations. He conducts workshops on personal and cultural development as a specialist in forming human connections. His mission is to use his God-given gifts to inspire and impact people dealing with adversity.

Learn more at
www.FrankEBrady.com

About the Authors

Derek Cradle was born and raised in White Plains, New York. After graduating from Delaware State University, he began his teaching career at William Henry Middle School in Dover, Delaware. He has been the principal of the High School of Sports Management since 2018. Previously, Mr. Cradle serviced students with special needs in kindergarten through twelfth grade classrooms for 24 years and was formerly the director of student life at the Academy of Arts and Letters in Fort Greene, Brooklyn.

Mr. Cradle is married to Monica and is the proud father of two daughters, Sydney Rosalouise and Logan Denise. He has been a proud member of Omega Psi Phi Fraternity Inc. since his initiation into the Psi Epsilon chapter at Delaware State University in the spring of 1994. Recently, Mr. Cradle was recognized by state senator Kevin Parker for his educational leadership. He is a proud member of Cornerstone Baptist Church in Brooklyn, New York.

To connect, email him
DCradle@schools.nyc.gov

Michael Rodriguez, Ed.D., a.k.a. "Dr. Rod" is a leading educational expert who works on issues of equity, diversity, leadership, and minority male development.

Michael has been highlighted by the City University of New York for his work within the Black Male Initiative Program, developing mentoring and leadership curriculums for African American and Latino males. He's been featured on the syndicated radio talk show, *The Tom Pope Show*, as well as radio broadcasts in the NYC area.

Michael comes from modest means and college became a way out. He seized that opportunity, changing the trajectory of his life. He is very passionate about helping others and dedicated his life to such, specifically to students from underserved communities, helping them use education as a tool to find success.

As a professional speaker, mentor, and founder of Empowering Minds for Tomorrow, he has spoken to thousands of students in numerous states and two countries.

Learn more at
www.dr-rod.com

Gerald Yarborough is an award-winning creative executive with extensive experience in the entertainment industry, as well as art direction and creative strategy related to film, television and kids' brands. A seasoned leader, Gerald has set direction and collaborated with creative professionals across numerous brands and lines of business, establishing new benchmarks in quality and design in the world of licensed consumer products.

In addition to creating and sustaining successful global campaigns for Viacom and Nickelodeon's consumer products, Gerald remains passionately engaged in arts education, philanthropic endeavors, and corporate social responsibility. He uses his experience and Viacom platform to motivate the next generation of creators of color. His active involvement in pro-social initiatives highlights the fact that he is not only an expert in his field, but an individual of outstanding character, integrity, and an example that no matter what background you come from, if you strive for excellence, there is no statistical bucket that can catch you.

To connect, email him at
Gerald.Yarborough@nick.com

H. Ato-Bakari Chase is an award-winning educator with over 20 years of successful experience. Specializing in urban and alternative education, Bro. Chase has successfully led, directed, or developed schools and educational programs especially for at-risk youth. He currently serves as the principal of the Blue Knights Academy Alternative Program in Irvington, New Jersey. He has also worked for the East Orange and Newark Public School Districts.

Along the way, Bro. Chase has received numerous accolades and accomplishments. He was named the Alternative Programs Teacher of the Year and he has been awarded the Pride in Public Education Award in recognition of his work by the East Orange Education Association. For directing and leading a successful male mentoring program, Bro. Chase was recognized by Ted Green, former councilman and current mayor of East Orange. Finally, Bro. Chase is a proud husband and a father to an amazing son.

To connect, email him at
atobakari@live.com

William Hodges was born and raised in the DM of the DMV. Educated in the D.C. and P.G. County, Maryland, school systems, he attended North Carolina A&T State University. He is the Creator of Bow Tie Willie's Bow Ties and Accessories.

William is a member of Reid Temple AME Church, where he serves as leader of the Boys to Men Mentoring Ministry and is a member of the Men's Council. His favorite Scripture is Psalm 37:23—"The steps of a good man are ordered by the Lord: and he delighteth in his way." Two of William's future projects include a men's lifestyle brand and the Live, Laugh, Love, and Pay Bills Couples Retreat.

William enjoys golfing; traveling; DIY projects; and his dogs, Ozzie and Eva. William is the son of Rev. Robert and Delores Hodges. He is married to Ayana and is the father of Alonnie. He resides in Baltimore, Maryland.

Learn more at
www.bowtiewillies.com

Horace L. Moore, an educator, youth advocate, and educational leader for over 28 years is also the founder and executive director of Chionesu Bakari (a mentorship program for young black men, ages 8 to 18 years old). Horace considers himself privileged to serve youth. He prides himself on being a knowledge leader on approaches to teaching and building positive young black males.

Born and raised in Brooklyn, New York, Horace is intimately aware of the challenges that face young black males in America, having navigated the path all of his life. He is grateful to be the product of a strong support system that taught him he was full of possibility. Horace firmly believes that when one is given the opportunity and encouragement to build on their God-given potential, there is little that they cannot accomplish. He is intent on providing those same opportunities to young black males of today.

Learn more at
www.youngblackmanonline.org

Frank N. Sanders is a retired Master Sergeant with over 22 years of service as a senior supply chain manager with the United States Army. He served in various military organizations throughout the US and overseas, including a tour of duty in Iraq from 2009-2010.

Frank's military awards include the Bronze Star Medal; three Meritorious Service Medals; eight Army Commendation Medals; and various unit awards, service medals, and ribbons. He was recognized for his exemplary career which epitomized the spirit, dignity, and sense of sacrifice and commitment of the United States Army. Frank's educational background includes a bachelor of arts in criminal justice from the University of Alaska, Anchorage, a bachelor of arts in sociology from William Paterson University, New Jersey, and a master of arts in transportation and logistics management from American Military University, Maryland.

Frank is a proven leader who is committed to excellence and driven to succeed by a strong sense of purpose.

To connect, email him at
frank.n.sanders1@gmail.com

Mendel Murray was born in Mount Vernon, New York. He is the youngest of three children born to Lloydette and James Murray. He credits his brother Devin and sister Nichelle with coaching him on how to be successful by being constant examples of hard work and determination.

Mendel graduated Summa Cum Laude from the University of Bridgeport and currently works for the Brooklyn Nets as a sales representative. He aspires to be an NBA executive, a career he has dreamed about since he was six years old.

Mendel is particularly proud of a project he created in honor of Black History Month entitled "The Untold," where he assisted in highlighting 28 distinguished but unsung African Americans who have contributed to their respective communities.

Today, Mendel continues to give back by making a difference in the lives of youth through his involvement with various mentoring programs in the Brooklyn and Bridgeport communities.

To connect, email him at
Mendel.murray@gmail.com

Randall E. Toby is a motivational speaker, career coach, and creator of the Breakfast with Our Boys series, an interactive two-hour conversation with male youth 12-18 years of age on topics important to their positive growth as men. Known for his high-energy speaking engagements, he is also the founder of the Magnificent Men Mentoring Group which provides workshops, group mentoring, and special events for middle school, high school, college students, and businesses. Born in Brooklyn, New York, he is currently a resident of Burlington, New Jersey.

Mr. Toby has been a guest speaker for Pelham Preparatory Academy/CFS, Camden Promise Neighborhood Center for Family Services, NYC Department of Probation, Westchester Community College State University of New York, West Philadelphia High School, and Burlington City High School to name a few. He is also a co-author of the bestselling book, *Suited for Success*, in which his chapter was "Let Your Situation Be Your Motivation."

To connect, email him at
mrtobyspeaks@gmail.com

Tony Simmons, very well known as DJ Tony Tone - The Blessed Kept Secret, is a national disc jockey and radio personality. This South Bronx native is the oldest of two children born to Carolyn and Willie Simmons. Tony's passion for music and people has allowed him to travel near and far with some of the biggest names in the entertainment industry. His style of delivering the gospel of Jesus Christ through music has influenced a generation of people from the youth to seniors.

Tony is a member of the world-famous Heavy Hitters; these DJs are proficient in all genres and can be found on TV, radio, and online. In February 2016, DJ Tony Tone made history as the very first DJ to host a gospel show on Hot 97, New York's top hip hop and urban contemporary radio station. You can hear Tony on Sunday mornings at 7:00 a.m.

To connect, email him at
tone@djtonytone.com

Barry J. Clark is a dynamic motivational public speaker with over 20 years of experience working in the human service and criminal justice field. Barry has worked with thousands of previously incarcerated men, women, and teenagers by teaching them career development, job readiness, and conflict resolution skills.

Barry uses the three E's: Educate, Enlighten, and Empower to promote what he believes is an indispensable principle of success. For over 20 years, he has had the honor of speaking at several prominent colleges, and conducting seminars at Rikers Island Correctional Facility, Fortune Society, and Abyssinian Baptist Church, as well as various community-based organizations.

In his current role as a senior account manager, Barry works with the Department of Probation and Parole, the Department of Homeless Services, and organizations who treat individuals with substance use disorders. He is also the director of community partnerships with the Magnificent Men Mentoring Group.

To connect, email him at
bjc_7111@yahoo.com

Frantz Condé is a masterful entrepreneur, educator, empowerment speaker, and entertainer. He is the founding president and CEO of Condé & Associates, Condé Global, and Condé Global Entertainment, using each platform to leverage his many talents and convert his passions into creative opportunities. Singing, songwriting, poetry, piano, creative storytelling, comedic improvisation, and professional hosting are his specialties.

Formerly a Fortune 500 analyst, Frantz currently creates pathways to financial independence through asset generation and leadership development. His dual master's degree in education is used to mentor underprivileged youth, demonstrating the power and process of self-discovery and servant-leadership. In addition, Frantz is also an aspiring honorary doctoral candidate at Morehouse College with the goal of becoming the world's greatest visionary artîste and creative storyteller par excellence. Establishing the Condé Global Foundation is also in the works, which will provide scholarships, mentorship, emotional support, guidance, and a roadmap for the successful transition from malehood to manhood.

To connect, email him at
condeglobal@gmail.com

Garry Smalley is a 25-year insurance veteran and entrepreneur born and raised in Brooklyn, New York. He studied finance at Virginia State University, then worked several jobs before he began his career at Geico. He touched all areas of insurance, moving from customer service to underwriting to Affinity program manager. He was responsible for negotiating exclusive marketing deals with University Alumni Association. In time, Garry created his consulting company to teach property and casualty insurance licensing classes. Soon after, he and two partners formed Fountain Risk Management. Within a few years, FRM was purchased by CoverWallet. Garry worked with CoverWallet for two years. He was soon offered a new opportunity to disrupt the real estate insurance industry and ElmSure, a wholly owned subsidiary of Roc Capital Holdings, was formed.

Garry is the father of two beautiful daughters and in his free time he mentors young men and women in the insurance industry.

To connect, email him at
gsmalley985@gmail.com

Larry Scott Blackmon leads FreshDirect's public affairs division. His work builds on FreshDirect's existing community and charitable partnerships across a variety of issues including fighting hunger, nutrition education, and career development. Larry brings nearly 20 years of public service, community development, and government experience to FreshDirect. He joined FreshDirect from the NYC Department of Parks and Recreation where he served as the deputy commissioner for community outreach.

In 2016-2018, Larry was recognized as one of the 50 most powerful community leaders in the Bronx and has been named one of the "40 under 40" people to watch in both the Network Journal and City and State publications.

Larry serves as a substitute professor for former New York City Mayor David Dinkins and has taught the mayor's public affairs course at Columbia University. Larry also serves Metropolitan College of New York as an adjunct professor.

To connect, email him at
Larry@blackmonllc.com

Norman Grayson is a savvy health advocate, entrepreneur, and ambassador of change who is on a lifelong mission to help people pave the path to longevity. His top priority is to create a legacy that will continue empowering others for generations.

Norman has received multiple awards and certificates from various esteemed ministries and entertainment groups. He currently serves as a founding member of a health and fitness company. He has also been involved with numerous ventures including radio interviews and speaking engagements, and he has co-authored two books—one currently an Amazon and *Black Enterprise* bestseller.

Norman enjoys dancing, quiet time, running his apparel and garment decorating business, going to the gym, yoga and meditation, and attending church. He is happily married and the proud father of three beautiful children. Above all, he cherishes nothing more than spending quality time with his wonderful family who inspires him to be his very best.

To connect, email him at
ngsaap2@gmail.com

Kenneth Wilson is an entrepreneur, strategist, and speaker from Silver Spring, Maryland. He is the CEO and principal consultant of Xsiban Enterprises, founder of the BMV Foundation, and co-founder of Black Squirrel Media. Kenneth was the recipient of the 2016 President's Lifetime Achievement Award. For over 15 years, Kenneth has worked in the fields of nonprofits, business, education, and local politics. He has held positions on every corporate level from volunteer and executive director to trustee member. He has also worked with individuals, families, and groups of all ages and backgrounds.

Kenneth's professional interests include project management, mentoring, and strategy. Kenneth has also been a passionate and active member in the community, serving as a mentor and connector for resources. You can listen to Kenneth as the host of the *Community Coalition Radio Show* and on YouTube as the host of *The Entrepreneur Life Show*.

Learn more at
www.xsibanenterprises.com/our-ceo

John Edwards has commanded large-scale complex workforce development programs and learning and development initiatives for more than 20 years. John holds a master's in public affairs and administration and a bachelor of science in systems analysis and computer programming. He has devoted his expertise to helping others advance and achieve their professional and personal goals.

Currently, John works for Metropolitan College of New York (MCNY) as the executive director of the Bronx Campus and College-Wide Career Development Initiatives. He is also an adjunct professor. Additionally, he is the co-founder and president of IManage Development, a learning and development consultant company.

John has proven to be a true servant-leader with an undeniable track record of success, and has an infectious enthusiasm aimed at helping others. A proud father of three young boys, John is a long-time resident of Brooklyn, New York, and was born in Panama City, Panama.

To connect, email him at
JEdwards@mcny.edu

Gregory Denizard is a vibrant leader and results ori-
ented professional with over twenty-five years of experience in nonprofit management and program administration. He has most recently served as the deputy
director of programs and operations for the Children's
Aid, an organization focused on helping children in
poverty to succeed and thrive.

Gregory is very active in the Hudson Valley
Westchester community. He is a head usher in his
church and is an active board member holding the vice
president position. Gregory and his wife, Michelle,
reside in Yonkers, New York, and are proud parents
of twelve-year-old son, Gregory, and fifteen-year-old
daughter, Kayla.

Currently, Gregory provides financial guidance
for clients, assisting them with making better decisions
regarding financial matters as it pertains to retirement
strategies, investments, asset preservation, and education funding. He oversees a leadership development
program in New Jersey and New York.

To connect, email him at
gdenizard@childrensaidnyc.org

Maurice L. Williams is a youth advocate, HBO/ABFF nominated short filmmaker, philanthropist, noted rap artist, journalist, entrepreneur, businessman, and rising national leader who is an inspiration and a role model for boys and young men faced with seemingly invincible odds. His life's work consists of the formulation of personal development workshops and manhood trainings for youth, particularly boys and young men of color.

As the founder of A Father's Love™ Mr. Williams has implemented his effective programs within three juvenile justice detention facilities across NYC. His aftercare, afterschool, summer camp, and re-entry programs are slated to begin in spring 2019 in the Harlem community. As a former juvenile delinquent from a single parent home, he knows firsthand what it takes to pull yourself up by the bootstraps.

Learn more at
www.afatherslove54.com

Milton Kelly is the author of three books and an advocate for mental health and affordable housing in NYC. He is a member of the NYC Suicide Prevention Council under Brett Scudder. Milton is currently a mental health peer counselor at Metropolitan Hospital-NYCHHC in New York City, in the section of East Harlem, where he works with clients in the mental health inpatient unit.

Milton is the recipient of the 2016 I Am Hope Humanitarian Award, and the 2017 and 2018 I Am Hope Breath Changers and Leadership Award. Milton Kelly currently lives in Brooklyn, New York, and is an active member at First Baptist Church of Crown Heights in Brooklyn, New York, where Reverend Dr. Darryl G. Bloodsaw is the pastor.

To connect, email him at
kellym209@gmail.com

Von Franklin, a black man and a refugee of Superstorm Sandy, returned to the South Bronx homeless and semi jobless in February of 2012. Mr. Franklin, a former ward of the state, learned how to organize folks in a group in the north Bronx. With no steady work in sight, Mr. Franklin began thinking about the legacy he would leave behind.

Mr. Franklin returned to familiar work as a community organizer with the New York City Housing Authority. The individuals there shared similar stories of their inabilities to afford advertisement that their businesses so desperately needed to go to the next level. Mr. Franklin created Mobile Office Media LLC to give small businesses and young and new entrepreneurs an affordable option, and to put a focus on stories and issues that the mainstream media outlets overlook.

To connect, email him at
Vonharveyfranklin@gmail.com

Jerry Francois was born and raised in Brooklyn, New York, to parents that emigrated from Haiti. Jerry grew up under strict family values and hard work ethics. With the spirit of an entrepreneur, he considers himself to be more of a conprenuer. To Jerry, a conprenuer is an ideology, a space that you arrive into. It is the person you can choose to become when graduating from prison.

Jerry is the CEO and founder of J&S Homes Enterprises, LLC, which he launched with his fiancée and COO, Stephelenecie Calixte, on June 1, 2019. As real estate investors, J&S will buy and hold residential and commercial properties.

To connect, email him at
Jerry.F@businessinaboxdirect.com

Hubert Lee Guy Jr. is a professionally licensed New York State master barber; barbering educator; actor; TV, fashion, and event host; recording artist; and, entrepreneur. Originally from Battle Creek, Michigan, he currently resides in Harlem, New York, and has three kids: Hubert, Daniel, and Nyimah.

Hubert is the CEO of Hubert Guy Grooming, which offers high end men's hair cutting, styling, and grooming. He is the head master barber for *The Marvelous Mrs. Maisel* and *The Code*, and he has styled hair on several TV shows, commercials, and videos. Hubert also teaches nationally for IATSE Local 798 Makeup Artists and Hair Stylists Union in New York. He produces and hosts his own TV show, *The Actors Cut*, and hosts different awards shows, fashion shows, and private events. He has been a featured actor in *Orange is the New Black*. He is also a recording artist and entrepreneur.

To connect, email him at
hubertguyjr@yahoo.com

CREATING DISTINCTIVE BOOKS
WITH INTENTIONAL RESULTS

We're a collaborative group of creative masterminds
with a mission to produce high-quality books to position
you for monumental success in the marketplace.

Our professional team of writers, editors, designers,
and marketing strategists work closely together to ensure
that every detail of your book is a clear representation
of the message in your writing.

Want to know more?
Write to us at info@publishyourgift.com
or call (888) 949-6228

Discover great books, exclusive offers, and more at
www.PublishYourGift.com

Connect with us on social media

@publishyourgift